Design Thinking for Program and Project Management

Understand Broadly
Empathize with Users
Define the Problem
Ideate, Prototype, Test, Iterate, and Build the Solution
Deploy to Users

Program/Project
Initiate
Define & Plan
Control & Monitor
Close & Next Steps

George Anderson, PhD, PMP

Design Thinking for Program and Project Management
Copyright © 2019 by George Anderson

ISBN-13: 978-1-697-41455-4
Library of Congress Control Number
First Published: October 2019
Printed in the United States of America

TRADEMARKS

WARNING AND DISCLAIMER

DEDICATION

This book is dedicated to my family and in particular to my
wife. I have seen her for years demonstrate empathy,
kindness, and grace towards others. She seeks to understand.
She listens deeply and embraces the kind of mindset that
pushes for change through little victories a day at a time. And
in doing so, she helps others get the hard things of life *done*.

In this way, my wife has been practicing the best of human-
centered *Design Thinking* well before I even knew the term. I
just thought of her approach as unconditional *love*.
Are they maybe one and the same?

I think they can be... Yes.

TABLE OF CONTENTS

TABLE OF FIGURES

Meet The Author

George Anderson is a Global Program Director for Microsoft Services and an Adjunct Professor and guest lecturer for several universities. George holds Stanford Innovation Leadership, Prosci Change Practitioner, and other certifications, alongside a PhD in Applied Management and an MBA.

As a Program Director, George builds and leads software teams that help organizations transform themselves. George's architects and consultants provide the technology and business skills necessary to design and develop transformational solutions, and George and his Project Managers provide the leadership and governance needed to deliver those solutions. In these ways, George's teams drive meaningful change and measurable value. It has never been easy work, and it has become more difficult as organizations have grown in complexity and reach. He's seen success, but he's seen unrealized transformations and outright failures as well.

George recognized that a different kind of approach to Program and Project Management was needed for the most complex or far-reaching Business and Operational Transformations. Regardless of the underlying software or technology solutions being deployed, the most common problems seemed to be solved faster through what George eventually realized were Design Thinking techniques. This understanding, combined with insights gained through Stanford's Innovation and Entrepreneurship Program, helped George iterate and finally settle on the *Design Thinking Model for Program and Project Management* shared here.

In March of 2019, George presented his perspectives to a local University interested in the intersection of Project Management and Design Thinking. This early work and subsequent feedback from that team sparked the genesis of this book. The following month, George invited his Program and Project Management colleagues to come together and discuss Design Thinking in the context of complex transformational change Programs. The team met weekly for several months, sharing ideas and real-world examples of Design Thinking in action.

Over the summer, George and two colleagues were asked to present their thoughts on transformational Program and Project "readiness" including guiding principles for organizing and mobilizing. Preparing for and iterating on this content influenced the book's Table of Contents and Design Thinking model while inspiring content for several chapters.

By the end of September, the book was content-complete, and it was edited and published the following month. The fact that this book was delivered in six months *concept-to-print* is a testament to the power of Design Thinking to improve time-to-value. More importantly, this book represents the ability of a team practicing Design Thinking to actually get hard things *done*... to *finish* something both complex and difficult... and in doing so, to quickly realize the value and benefits of their effort.

Acknowledgements

There are so many people to thank! I first want to call out my family for their awesome love, help, and reassurance; Keri Porter and her team of academics and professionals for their early curiosity, thinking, and feedback which grew and shaped this book; and Paul MacDonald and Shaily Nair for their strong support of this effort after hours.

In addition to my hard-working copy editors and creative cover design consultants, I also want to thank the following team of business and program leaders, project managers, transformation experts, technology and business solution specialists, content contributors, reviewers, and fellow Design Thinking enthusiasts:

David Driftmier, General Manager for the Americas and long-time Business Applications leader who was gracious enough to author the Foreword. David's tremendous support over the years, his ability to create outstanding work environments, and his empathy for customers models the best of both Servant Leadership and Design Thinking.

Rebecca Whitworth, Program Director who served in a Chief Editor and Reviewer role for much of the content and its organization. Rebecca was a great source of encouragement throughout the authoring process. She contributed significant content and thinking spanning a number of chapters as well, in particular Chapter 9, *Mobilizing for Effectiveness*, and Chapter 10, *Executing and Realizing Value*.

Luis Solano, Program Director and Design Thinking enthusiast who shared Design Thinking tenets and techniques reflected in Chapter 1, *Why Design Thinking?*, and Chapter 2, *What is Design Thinking?*.

Suresh Gopalakrishnan, Senior Project Manager who provided content and feedback for both Chapter 2, *What is Design Thinking?*, and Chapter 3, *Program and Project Management Basics*.

Colin Silveira, Senior Project Manager who provided content and feedback for Chapter 2, *What is Design Thinking?*, and a review of Chapter 4, *Simple Rules and Guiding Principles*.

Stephen Wilson, Program Director and Design Thinking enthusiast who provided thinking and techniques that were incorporated into Chapter 5, *Communications*, and Chapter 8, *Program and Project Planning*.

Sharon Long, Senior Project Manager who provided early thinking and techniques reflected in Chapter 6, *Drawing on and Shaping Culture*.

Brent Hawkinson, Program Director and senior technologist who provided context and thinking that informed Chapter 7, *Creating and Running Collaborative Teams*.

Dave Spear, Senior Delivery Manager who provided early thinking and significant content and feedback for Chapter 7, *Creating and Running Collaborative Teams*, and Chapter 9, *Mobilizing for Effectiveness*.

Gretchen Peaco, Senior Project Manager who provided early thinking and content for Chapter 1, *Why Design Thinking?*, and Chapter 9, *Mobilizing for Effectiveness*.

Michael Herold, **Steve Kearl**, **Ali Aksut**, and **Mahesh Tej Vupasi**, Senior Business Consultants, Functional experts, and Design Thinking enthusiasts who provided a cross-section of epic ideas and techniques informing Chapter 10, *Executing and Realizing Value*.

Rick Furino, Program Director and long-time mentor who provided early perspectives around what it means to deliver complex Programs and Projects. Rick's expert guidance spans Chapter 10, *Executing and Realizing Value*, and Chapter 11, *Governing, Controlling, and Monitoring*.

Peter Dordoy, Program Director who reviewed Chapter 12, *Confirming Value, Closing, and Next Steps*, and provided broad-based thinking and feedback spanning several other chapters including Appendix B, *Design Thinking Techniques*.

The practical experience of this extraordinary team of thinkers and advisors created much of the enduring value of this book. Numerous customers and partners helped shape this content as well. Together, this team demonstrated the value of iteration and collaboration, lived out the adage that few things of real value are ever completed solo, and reaffirmed my long-held belief that we can accomplish anything when we lean on God (Phil 4:13) and on one another. I am blessed beyond measure to know and have the opportunity to work with each of you.

Thank you.

Foreword

Every day in companies around the world, IT organizations and their business partners are striving to align technology with business needs in order to produce positive outcomes. These outcomes include faster time to market, improved margins, streamlined supply chains, and better products, to name but a few. As laudable as these goals are, we should all be shifting our focus to the *people* served by technology and their larger organizations and systems.

> *Design Thinking, in the way it is laid out in this book,*
> *then becomes a timeless outcomes-enabler and not*
> *simply the latest technology or management fad.*

It is through focusing on people and their needs that we can best deliver these outcomes. Design Thinking is ultimately in service to people, after all, and not simply processes and outcomes, thereby transcending trends and temporary patterns we see come and go.

George is intimately familiar with the scenarios that create challenges for both business and IT. While he uses his deep experience to add valuable insights in the chapters that follow, the real value of his experience is how he has not only adopted Design Thinking as a personal tool for success, but has translated those concepts and techniques into actions that have resulted in some of the most impactful and transformative Programs and Projects at several of the world's largest companies.

Business books often do a brilliant job of framing a well-known challenge to the point where the reader exclaims, "Yes! Exactly!" Too frequently, however, the successive chapters fail to deliver an enduring solution to the problem that was so well laid out. *Design Thinking for Program and Project Management* provides both the tools and the foundation for the mind shift that needs to occur to create human-centric solutions necessary to solve the tough business problems of tomorrow. George lays out an approach and a path that those of us at the crossroads of business and technology would be wise to follow.

David Driftmier
General Manager, Americas

Introduction

"The key to everything is empathy, because nothing is more effective and fruitful than the ability to walk in the shoes of others."

—Satya Nadella

Completing the Complex and Unique

Complexity, ambiguity, and time are among the greatest enemies to solving hard problems. Whether you are tasked to construct the Empire State Building in under 14 months or deliver a critical global business transformation across 3 years, completing large-scale unique endeavors takes time. As complexity and ambiguity increase, the need for more time increases... and so too does the need for deeper empathy, stronger leadership, and the willingness to experiment, take risks, and learn.

Organizing people and resources to solve and deliver solutions for these complex problems is the work of Program and Project Management. And truth be told, the experts who lead such work should have it easy. After all, they can follow a formula of mature and well-understood processes to generally deliver a body of work on time and on budget.

So why do so many complex Programs and Projects fail (Cobb, 1995)? And of the few that manage to deliver what they promised, why are so many of these Programs and Projects late? Worse, why do the benefits promised by too many of these endeavors either dry up along the way or never materialize at all? It seems we have a time-to-value crisis.

Solving difficult and unique problems will always be incredibly hard. Leading and delivering large-scale business transformations and complex technology-enabled solutions will always be hard, too. Nearly fifty years ago, Rittel and Webber (1973) described these tough endeavors as *wicked problems*. Such problems are wicked in the sense they seem insanely difficult to solve. Their environments are ambiguous and fluid, making the problems difficult to define with certainty. Potential solutions are subsequently unclear and notoriously incomplete. In light of these challenges, solutions to wicked problems require changes not only in how people think but in how they operate. To paraphrase Einstein, such problems cannot be solved with the same mindset that created them.

What makes delivering solutions to super complex and uniquely wicked problems as difficult as ever today? How can we solve hard problems in a

13

world where patience is thin and expectations only continue to rise? Our experience gives us some insight into these questions and needs:

- **Managing expectations.** Solving complex problems is not about achieving perfect solutions today, but rather about incrementally learning and using those learnings to improve imperfect solutions over time. If leaders insist on perfect solutions, and users expect the same, nothing will ever get done.

- **Understanding.** From a big-picture perspective, if the team cannot describe the environment underpinning a problem, they may misunderstand it altogether and solve the wrong problem.

- **Empathy.** If the team does not deeply understand the needs of the people who will be using a solution, including how they will use it, the solution itself might not solve the problem at all.

- **Ambiguity.** Understanding the real problem to be solved takes time and a willingness to wade through ambiguity. Teams must be comfortable with "learning and failing and learning and failing" as they work to seek greater understanding and clarity.

- **Process alignment.** Complex problem definition and solutioning demands ideating, prototyping, and iterating, none of which are optional; the goal is to learn fast, refine a team's understanding of both the problem and its potential solutions, and iterate.

- ***Build to Think* mentality.** Complex problems cannot be solved exclusively by "thinking and planning." Instead, the team also needs permission and direction to *build and try and do* on their journey to more deeply understanding and learning.

- **Diversity by Design.** Teams must be designed to be diverse in thought, background, and experience. Homogenous teams are limited in their thinking and therefore in their capacity to ideate and innovate. If diversity is absent, Step One is solving that diversity problem.

- **Trust and Cultural Intelligence.** Trying and doing, followed by failing and learning, takes trust, courage, and cultural awareness or intelligence. Teams that do not trust one another cannot do the hard work of transparent ideation or selfless collaboration, and they will never, ever, be truly successful.

- **Human-centric Leadership.** If human-centric governance, communications, and feedback are inadequate, or the team has been denied the necessary time, support, and tools for learning and iterating, the final work products and other transformational outcomes will also be inadequate.

Based on the insight above, it is necessary to evolve the management and governance techniques used by leaders supporting the teams working through the "trying and doing" in search of solutions. Those who are leading, equipping, managing, and governing need to iteratively learn just as their teams must do. Leaders who do not aggressively push themselves to adopt new techniques, who do not fully support their teams to think and learn quickly by doing and failing quickly, and who do not set realistic expectations with Sponsors, stakeholders, users, and others, will never help their teams solve the hardest problems.

*Complex problem-solving requires arming the problem solvers as well as **those who lead the problem solvers** with a special set of techniques.*

These teams need to operate in both a programmatic and flexible manner, refining techniques borrowed from standard Program and Project Management practices and human-centric disciplines. Our conclusion is simple: Complex problem solving and solutioning calls for *Design Thinking-inspired Program and Project Management.*

If time is our enemy, Design Thinking is our response. A human or user-centric way of operating gives the entire team—from Sponsors and stakeholders to managers, business leads, architects, developers, and users—the permission, alignment, and guidelines needed to think differently and deliver faster. Design Thinking provides many of the tools and techniques needed to work through complex problems. It facilitates understanding an environment broadly; empathizing with the users operating within that environment; defining those users' needs and problems; prototyping and testing potential solutions; quickly learning from and iterating on those potential and partial solutions to build a viable initial solution; and finally delivering and deploying that viable solution to users *with the intention of iterating further*, knowing full well that waiting on a perfect solution is neither practical nor desirable.

Applying Design Thinking to Programs and Projects

To dramatically improve success rates and time-to-value, a fundamental change in thinking is called for. That change is found in human-centric Design Thinking. In this book, we apply more than 70 Design Thinking techniques to standard Program and Project Management processes. We explore the tensions between delivering quickly versus delivering fully; delivering value through iterations and incremental updates versus delaying that value through long cycles of planning; and building upon minimally viable solutions versus trying to deliver perfect solutions.

We focus on learning as we walk through the phases of a Program or Project, applying Design Thinking techniques and principles along the way. We point out where employing these techniques to tried and true Program and Project Management processes yields better results faster.

Some might label this approach as agile or innovative. Truth be told, it is really about letting go of long-held Program and Project Management doctrine and striking out in new ways. The new ways may be different to many Program and Project leaders, but they are actually not new at all; our Design colleagues have been using them for years. These new ways might feel risky at times, too, but using Design Thinking techniques in fact helps reduce the risk of outright Program or Project failure.

For our purposes, delivering transformational outcomes and solutions to complex problems means:

- Modifying standard Program and Project Management tasks and processes—those that we wrap around building and delivering a solution or transformation—with Design Thinking techniques.

- Drawing on these Design Thinking-inspired management tasks and processes—and the *Build to Think* culture they promote—to develop and deploy solutions to hard problems faster.

All of the Design Thinking techniques explored throughout the book are outlined in Appendix B, *Design Thinking Techniques*, starting on p. 196.

Speed rather than Perfection

Consider the effect of diminishing returns when introducing something new. Because doing something new means change, new is painful. But change and therefore pain is really the only road to long-term longevity; there's no way around it. The key is to get started on the change (and yes, ensure the change is adopted). There are plenty of once-solid organizations that ultimately revealed it's not smart to ignore the need to change or to put off the time to change. Think about the stories of Sears, Borders, Blockbuster, Yahoo, Blackberry, RadioShack, Circuit City, Toys R Us, Kodak, Xerox, Hostess, TiVo, and others (Aaslaid, 2018).

On the other hand, there are a great many examples of broad and yet painful innovation, reinvention, and transformation *success stories*, too— consider Amazon, Netflix, New York's Empire State Building, Microsoft, Uber, Tesla, Google, Apple, and more.

*These success stories prove that starting off as an online bookseller or DVD retailer or proposed 25 story office building does not limit us or keep us from changing and striving and **becoming** more.*

What is really interesting about these success stories is that they are not flawless execution stories. Their transformation journeys are littered with false starts, revised plans, and just plain ol' bad ideas. But in all of these cases, organizational and Program/Project leaders tried and failed and yet *learned fast enough* to course-correct. They didn't get everything perfect the first time, *but they got enough directionally right fast enough* for their respective transformations to succeed.

More than 95% of the Fortune 500 have active business transformation programs in place today. In such a world, then, the true transformation differentiator can become time-to-value as much as the actual solution being delivered; after all, slow transformation, like slow innovation, yields little competitive advantage, delays new revenues, and drives higher rather than lower overall costs.

An even more important transformation differentiator lies in actually completing the transformation. The idea here is to transform not only in a directionally accurate kind of way, but to pursue it with speed and to *finish*. If time is the real enemy, how will you transform faster than your competitors or faster than you might otherwise be capable? By drawing from a tool bag of proven Design Thinking techniques, and in doing so changing the way in which you *manage* and *execute* to solve problems and deliver solutions. In the end, then, how and where you apply Design Thinking and its techniques will actually become your key differentiator as you deliver value along the way and *complete* the hard work of transformation itself.

Why this Book?

Delivering a business or operations transformation Program or Project is not just a huge piece of work but an enormous investment. We will help you consider and explore new ways of thinking and working through ambiguity every step of the way. We will teach you where and how to boldly sidestep standard practices or incremental change in favor of strategic revolution, and when to stick with the standard or incremental because they actually get you to the Finish Line faster. We will share with you what others typically do and explain how you might strive to do the same thing faster and with greater benefit to your users...

... and we will show you how to gain a competitive edge as you employ Design Thinking and its various techniques as a strategy for delivering Program and Project outcomes faster.

Velocity will play a central role in your strategy, and paradoxically so will failure... little failures that lead to learning and understanding, and ultimately to velocity. Your strategic foundation will comprise strong communications practices, diversity-founded collaborative teaming, and superior cultural awareness and intelligence because as Peter Drucker is attributed to saying, "Culture eats strategy for breakfast." You will learn how to draw on your current culture for initial progress while shaping that culture for future effectiveness and greater organizational longevity. You will change the very way in which your teams seek to understand, empathize, think, and operate, and you will employ Simple Rules and Guiding Principles to help drive smarter transformation decisions and consistent execution. Finally, you will learn how to effectively mobilize and execute, and in parallel how to effectively govern, control, and monitor your progress in ways that increase clarity and deliver results.

And you will Finish what many others never do.

Why Us?

With tremendous combined breadth and depth of experience, look to us as part of your extended team. We have navigated the same waters and walked the same paths you are facing. We have already made the mistakes you wish to avoid, and we are excited to share our experience.

Throughout these pages, we will equip you to think
and operate differently.

In this way, you will eventually make fewer missteps and cross the Finish Line faster. You will deliver real value sooner than you would have achieved using standard Program and Project Management processes.

You will still know the pain that comes with running large change-enabling Programs and Projects. But by understanding and putting your users first—at the center of everything—while applying the Design Thinking techniques covered here, you will realize time-to-value and other benefits that more than make up for the pain of change.

Our Audience and Approach

If you lead, manage, deliver, equip others, or in other ways help support large or complex Programs and Projects, you will find this book useful. That includes:

- Program and Project Managers and other Delivery leaders
- End users, especially those tasked with helping to brainstorm, design, evaluate, and test new solutions
- Executives, Sponsors, and other transformation leaders
- Business managers and analysts
- Innovation and design specialists
- Change management specialists
- Architects and consultants
- Training specialists and other educators
- System support and operations specialists
- Students of Design Thinking and anyone interested in learning what it means to apply Design Thinking principles to a specific discipline so as to apply similar thinking or techniques elsewhere.

We never intended to create a Program or Project Management text, but the book doesn't stray far from standard practices (see Chapter 3, *Program and Project Management Basics*, p. 50). With several exceptions that we note along the way, know that we have aligned our work to the Project Management Institute's sixth edition of the PMBOK®, *A Guide to the Project Management Body of Knowledge*, published in 2017.

A key strength of this Design Thinking book is that it reflects a balance of breadth and depth of material to satisfy beginners, intermediate readers, and long-time Program and Project experts. In this way, every chapter is *consumable* for every reader. For beginners to Program and Project Management or Design Thinking in particular, read this Introduction and the first three chapters sequentially. If you're more experienced, you will find it easy to skip around and explore chapters as you like but be sure to read foundational Chapters 1, 2, and 4 at a minimum. To keep you engaged and less distracted, we have incorporated content-specific heatmaps and figures and have spelled out most acronyms again and again in each chapter (rather than only the first time they're introduced); we hope you find these practices useful.

Because Design Thinking is by no means exclusive to a particular type of Program or Project or methodology, you will find that this book works well across a range of industries or software solutions. Our experience spans technology and software business applications from Microsoft, SAP, NetSuite, Oracle, Sage, Infor, and others, as well as a number of custom application development platforms. You will see as we have seen that Design Thinking and its techniques work equally well regardless of software vendor or business solution. Any complex endeavor benefits from human-centric thinking.

Wherever complex and unique problems abound, and obvious solutions are elusive, call upon the more than 70 Design Thinking techniques and methods applied throughout the book.

Organizing the Book

This book is organized into three high-level sections called *Parts* that follow standard Program and Project Management phases:

- Part One, *Setting the Stage*, lays the groundwork for the book and comprises the first four chapters. Here we complete an introduction and explain the "why" and "what" of Design Thinking. Then we walk through standard Program and Project Management basics. We conclude Part One with a discussion on the role and purpose of Design Thinking's Simple Rules and Guiding Principles.

- Part Two, *Getting Ready*, focuses initially on the foundational elements of communications and culture. Then we turn our attention to creating effective and collaborative teams. We conclude Part Two with a walk-through of Program and Project planning followed by matters of mobilization and general readiness.

- Part Three, *Executing at Speed*, covers the hard work of running a Program or Project in a way that realizes benefits and outcomes faster than traditionally possible. We work through the tension between executing repeatably and iterating to learn and improve. We then review what it means to govern, control, and monitor. The final chapter concludes with the work necessary to confirm realized value, close out the Program or Project, and think through Next Steps.

What Is Not Covered

Although we cover Program and Project Management in reasonable detail in Chapter 3, we do not explore the minutia of knowledge areas, process groups, and so on. Again, look to guidance from the Project Management Institute (2017) for details. In addition, though we speak broadly of business applications and solutioning throughout the book, we never intended to provide specific software and services advice, nor did we ever wish to align around a particular software suite or implementation methodology; again, Design Thinking is neither bound by nor limited by software or technology vendors and their methodologies.

We are not here to consider applying Design Thinking to creating business solutions as much as we are focused on applying Design Thinking to the **management and governance processes** *necessary to actually deliver that business solution smarter and faster as part of a broader Program or Project.*

Real-world Lessons and Design Thinking Techniques

When we initially discussed this book project, we agreed it was important to share the lessons we have collectively learned over the years as we sought (with varying success) to accelerate complex multi-year business application, operational, and organizational transformations. For this reason, we have included real-world lessons, real-life explanations, common mistakes you need to avoid, a rich Appendix of Design Thinking techniques applied here and in practice, and much more. In our view, material like this creates a worthwhile and *usable* reference.

We also wanted to provide a mechanism for applying what you're reading in a way that really brings it all together. To this end, each chapter concludes with an ongoing fictional case study with questions and answers. The questions are not difficult but should help reinforce the content. The case study itself is an amalgamation of many different Programs and Projects and includes common challenges and questions which highlight each chapter's material.

In conclusion, our experiences are real, gleaned from a mix of global Programs and smaller yet still complex Projects across a breadth of industries. The impact that Design Thinking has had in solving wicked problems and getting hard things done is real as well. Thank you again for adding this book to your collection.

PART I

Setting the Stage

Chapter 1

Why Design Thinking?

Welcome to Design Thinking for Program and Project Management!

Executing large-scale business overhauls and organizational transformations continues to be one of the most prevalent undertakings in commercial and public organizations alike. Such Programs and Projects enable organizations to change how they go to market or operate and serve others. In doing so, these organization seek to not only remain viable but to improve current business capabilities, introduce new capabilities, reduce costs, enhance competitiveness, and more.

> *Based on the sheer number of new business transformations started in the last several years, smart organizations believe that the reward outweighs the effort. A big part of this effort and cost is in the form of the overhead necessary to manage and deliver those business transformations.*

Program and Project Management, or P&PM, acts as a wrapper surrounding these in-flight organizational and business changes. This wrapper safeguards and protects. And it helps ensure that the change-enabling components of a transformation are indeed designed, developed, and deployed. Without Program and Project Management, there *is* no business transformation.

The work of Program and Project Management is broad. It includes all of the processes and tasks and people necessary to help an organization's business professionals, change management experts, IT professionals, and so many others support the teams that designing and delivering the new business capabilities. It is easy to see how attention to design and people's needs would be useful for this team.

But what about the Program and Project Management team? Surely, they should benefit from attention to design and to people's needs, too. In the real world of Program and Project Management, the lines between the solution being developed and the overhead necessary to support that development are blurred.

Like a protective sheath around a power cord, good
Program and Project Management wraps up and
protects the transformational work being delivered.

Program and Project Management serves as the protective sheath and insulator, while the business transformation is akin to the interior wires delivering the Program's or Project's value and power (see Figure 1.1).

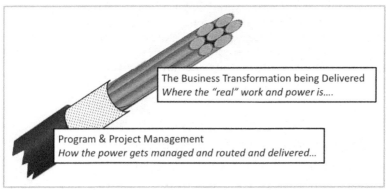

The Business Transformation being Delivered
Where the "real" work and power is....

Program & Project Management
How the power gets managed and routed and delivered...

Figure 1.1 Program and Project Management governs, routes, and delivers the Power.

Beyond a wrapper or sheath, another way we can view P&PM is through the lens of a Database Management System. P&PM work and tasks are analogous to the *meta work* surrounding the "real work" of a business transformation, in the same way that *meta data* helps describe and support the data held in a database, data warehouse, or data lake. The two must co-exist together; neither will ever deliver value alone.

Overcoming the Perils Along the Way

Business transformations and other large change endeavors simply cannot happen without formal Program and Project Management. The oversight and overhead are not optional. P&PM provides the necessary supervision, discipline, stakeholder expectation management, schedule and scope management, and control. In the end, Program and Project Management makes a business transformation possible.

Like a good roadmap, Program and Project Management paves the way for managing the delivery of a solution. The roadmap describes not only the path outlining how to get from here to there but also the obvious and hidden risks and potential pitfalls (see Figure 1.2). From sponsorship, contracting, and staffing issues to challenges and opportunities associated with communications, culture, and more, we will cover these and other Perils throughout the book. More importantly, we will look at ways to apply and infuse Design Thinking to help overcome these Perils.

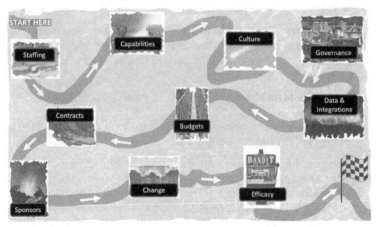

Figure 1.2 The complex Program/Project journey and a sampling of its Perils.

Several of the Perils associated with complex and large-scale business transformation Programs and Projects that can be better facilitated or managed through Design Thinking include (in no real order):

- The **Staffing Sand Trap**, which keeps the team from moving forward until core team roles are assembled; it takes the core team to get out of the trap.

- The **Capability Chasm** or Cliff, which prematurely stops the team from delivering until the Program has the right people with the right skills at the right time. Solid team capabilities serve as a bridge to get us over a countless number of chasms and cliffs along the way.

- The **Culture Comet**, which keeps coming back to bite us if we fail to draw on our current culture and actively work in parallel to shape it. Organizational culture, project-team work climate, and individual culture need to be understood and shaped early to maximize productivity, innovation, and the ability to effectively apply Design Thinking to ideate, solve problems, and work through challenges.

- **Distractions** due to poor **Governance** practices, the net of which ultimately frees the Program or Project team to wander off and lose focus. Armed with strong governance processes and practices, the PMO provides the adult supervision necessary to keep the teams and the Program or Project moving forward.

- **Data and Integrations Firestorms** start early; the potential for data issues and integration failures (between our Program and its underlying Component Projects and other projects) to stall and smolder for months and finally burst into flames means these perils need constant (and early) attention and control; further, the complexity of these efforts nearly always demands they be treated as Component Projects.

- The **Funding and Budget Bridge**, which slows us down and can quickly halt everything; Programs and Projects need not only initial funding, but they need budgets earmarked for inevitable changes down the road, too.

- The **Contracts Mudslide**, which also comprises licensing and other such paperwork can quickly slow everyone down and render completed work useless in the same way that a mudslide stops an entire caravan in its tracks.

- The **Sponsorship Volcano**, which can be on the verge of blowing at any time, making visible and active sponsorship necessary from the start of a Program or Project; good Sponsors and sponsorship help us navigate inevitable lava flows as well.

- A series of **Change Waves**, which sneak up deadly quiet every time we tweak a process or institute new standards and procedures; like a tidal wave, these change waves threaten to wipe away all of our good work unless the change is managed and adopted and reinforced effectively.

- The **Efficacy Bandits** or **Blockers**, which rob a Program or Project of the ability to finish well if at all; common efficacy bandits include poor leadership and communications, ineffective processes, rules, and principles, and a lack of attention to change and culture, all of which quietly conspire to make it nearly impossible to get hard things done.

Why Design Thinking? Flexibility and Freedom

Let's get back to the matter at hand—why Design Thinking for Program and Project Management? For starters, we know that conventional Program and Project management does not give us the permission or flexibility we may need in terms of how to work to solve big problems. Nor does conventional P&PM help us wade through the inevitable ambiguity, figure out the right problems to solve, or give us the freedom to try and fail and try again. Instead, conventional P&PM is about following a set of basic rules, standards, and practices.

Conventional Program and Project Management reinforces process repeatability, rigid gates, quality checkpoints, and other such practices. And to be clear, these are all great things when the problem and solution are evident, and the solution simply needs to be planned and delivered.

We need something better—a smarter approach—if we expect to overcome the Perils of a complex and unique Program or Project. As you have already guessed, this is where Design Thinking-inspired Program and Project Management comes into play.

Applying Design Thinking to proven P&PM processes still allows us to leverage the repeatability and predictability from those proven processes. But when and where needed, Design Thinking also gives us the methods, freedom, and flexibility to tackle unknowns and to learn and iterate. In the end, Program and Project Management practices informed by Design Thinking therefore help us *deliver*, discussed next.

Why Design Thinking? Reducing Time and Cost

Through our learnings and intentional course corrections, Design Thinking-inspired Program and Project Management helps us navigate the Perils and arrive at the Finish line faster than we otherwise would. And because we arrive faster, we save money not only in terms of the staff and resources that we can cut loose early but also because we avoid many of the pitfalls that would have taken us down costly sidetracks, stalls, and dead ends.

Why Design Thinking? Realizing Value Faster

Maximizing freedom and flexibility is important, as is improving clarity. And reducing costs and risks will always be coveted outcomes, too.

For most organizations, arguably the best answer to the question "Why Design Thinking?" lies in the notion of much-improved Time-to-Value.

By getting to the Finish Line of a business transformation Program or Project faster, we setup an organization to begin more quickly realizing the value of the solutions they've invested so much time in managing and delivering. Better yet, deftly and intentionally applied Design Thinking can help organizations realize incremental value *along the way*, well before a Program or Project concludes.

The Struggle: Balancing the Tension

Design Thinking is also about balancing the tension between running fast and running slower but consistently. Just as the tortoise can occasionally beat the hare, Design Thinking doesn't rob us of the opportunity to choose repeatability and predictability. Repeatability and predictability might very well be the smart decision or the right answer. Repeatability allows us to move with precision (and potentially at a nice pace), knowing if we execute in the same way over and over we will likely wind up at an expected place with an expected outcome time and time again.

And we might *need* to go slower at times to be sure we do not miss key requirements or start without the necessary groundwork in place. Similarly, we may want to leverage repeatable P&PM processes when those processes yield the right outcomes at the best cost or lowest risk.

On the other hand, an organization's need for improved time-to-value will guide us in other situations to go faster, learn faster, prototype and innovate, and get something done faster than usual, even if the "something" represents an incremental solution for now. Practicing good Design Thinking is about understanding when we need to change our processes to pursue clearer problem definition or more effective solutioning, and when we instead need to choose predictability.

Point-in-Time Thinking: Best and Common Practices

In most walks of life, there is talk of leveraging "best" practices to reduce risks or deliver faster and cheaper by learning from others. After all, for every thousand Programs or Projects, there are probably hundreds of paths available to achieve at least *some* level of success.

But there are perhaps only several *really good* ways or a single *best* way to achieve success. These preferred paths are earmarked as *best practices*—the one or two best or preferred methods of doing a particular task, or addressing a particular problem, or executing a particular process. It is these nuggets of predictable and hard-learned point-in-time insight and knowledge that have helped many a Program or Project make at least some progress down the road to success.

Outside of the one or two *best* practices for doing something exists a set of potentially many *common* ways of doing the same thing.

> *Common Practices stand apart from Best Practices in one important way: they strike a more cost-effective balance between what is best and what is acceptable.*

Common practices are not as effective as best practices, but they are cheaper. The classic trade-off cited by those executing common practices over best practices lies in sacrificing capabilities or qualities or even time for reduced costs; common practices are nearly always much less expensive than best practices. We like to say that common practices fall into the bucket of **Good Enough**, delivering close to the same capabilities or quality than best practices, but at lower cost. It is also commonplace to see common practices implemented faster than best practices, but again by delivering fewer capabilities or lower quality.

The key to choosing common practices over best practices is to understand where your appetite for risk or diminishing returns lies. If you can achieve X at the 95th percentile and at half the cost of achieving your X's planned goal of 96%, and 95% is acceptable to your users, then you have a good case for implementing X using less-costly *common practices* rather than "better" but more costly *best practices*.

Longer-Term Thinking: Simple Rules and Guiding Principles

In the end, best practices and common practices are super valuable but they represent a point in time. This time constraint is their limitation.

Best and common practices change over time...as the environment changes, staffing models change, financials change, business changes, or technology changes. Best practices in designing and implementing high speed cloud storage systems change every year, for example, as does practices for managing, cultivating, and thinking about differences in culture, styles in leadership, user interfaces for phones, integrating systems of record into cohesive solutions, and countless other areas.

A longer-term and more sustainable approach to
faster decisioning and clearer strategy can be found
in creating Simple Rules and Guiding Principles.

Develop and apply Simple Rules to your team or program or project end-to-end. These rules define who you are, what's important, what's not, what you will create or do, what and who you will connect and work with, and perhaps rules related to timing or priorities. These rules number less than ten (something closer to six is ideal), and they become your guidepost or formula for executing. Simple Rules help define and govern your strategy, too, explored more in Chapter 4 starting on p. 62.

Where Simple Rules define the Who and What and When, Guiding Principles define the How. Guiding Principles outline how you will operate, how you will think, how you will prioritize, and more; they give us the guardrails necessary to make smart decisions quickly and in alignment with our Simple Rules and overall strategy. See Figure 1.3 for a view into how Best and Common Practices work alongside Simple Rules and Guiding Principles.

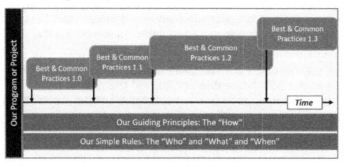

Figure 1.3 Point-in-Time Practices vs longer-term Rules and Principles.

Unlike best and common practices, our Simple Rules and Guiding Principles are intended to survive over the long-term... until you change the focus of your team, workstream, Project, or Program. Because they're so central to both Design Thinking and to execution, most of our chapters conclude with a set of Guiding Principles useful to help organize and think through that chapter's central themes.

Chapter Summary

This first chapter set the stage for applying Design Thinking in the context of solving the kinds of hard (in terms of complexity, ambiguity, time, and resourcing) problems tackled by standing up and managing large-scale Programs and Projects. Design Thinking was positioned as a key enabler for realizing value faster, all the while acknowledging the struggle we face between iterating and learning quickly vs establishing repeatability and therefore predictability and quality.

We concluded this first chapter by taking a closer look at the limitations of Best and Common practices, including introducing the notion of developing and using longer-term Simple Rules and Guiding Principles (which are further detailed throughout Chapter 4 starting on p. 62).

All of the Design Thinking techniques explored here and elsewhere are outlined in Appendix B, *Design Thinking Techniques*, starting on p. 196.

Chapter Case Study

You have been retained by the executive committee of your employer, Falcon Advanced Shipping and Transport (FAST), to introduce new business capabilities into the firm's shipping operations. FAST is in the midst of replacing and augmenting a host of business applications and other capabilities across its 22 worldwide locations spanning three continents. Called Program Harmony, this global business transformation effort comprises three Component Projects: Customer Connections Management (CMM), Shipping for Velocity (S4V), and Analytics for Business (A4B).

The board was impressed with your perspective on business and operations transformation efforts, particularly in terms of how Program and Project Management (P&PM) can benefit from the same kinds of design-focused thinking typically applied to creating and delivering new solutions. The CEO in particular is supportive of fine tuning and adjusting their standard Program and Project Management processes. He is hopeful that doing so will help FAST more quickly reimagine and deliver innovative business outcomes.

To help ground the executive committee, the CEO has requested that you host a Q&A session to answer several of the committee's questions surrounding Design Thinking for Program and Project Management.

Chapter 1: Questions

1. How should we think about the Solutions that we might inform through Design Thinking versus the Program and Project Management surrounding the development and delivery of those Solutions?

2. What are five of the many potential perils associated with large-scale business transformation Programs and Projects that we would expect to encounter and presumably defeat through Design Thinking?

3. In what way does Design Thinking give our standard Program and Project Management processes and methods freedom and flexibility?

4. What is the real value and answer to the question "Why Design Thinking?" for Program and Project Management?

5. From a time-frame or time horizon perspective, what is the difference between Best/Common Practices and Simple Rules/Guiding Principles?

See Appendix A starting on p. 187 for Case Study answers.

Chapter 2

What is Design Thinking?

In this Chapter, we build on *Why Design Thinking* outlined earlier in Chapter 1 and explore what Design Thinking comprises, including understanding the big picture, gaining empathy, defining problems, ideating, prototyping, testing and iterating, and deploying a solution. Then we explore Design Thinking techniques and strategies, concluding with a set of Guiding Principles for human centered or user-centric thinking. Note that the various terms formatted in **bold** represent Design Thinking techniques, steps, or approaches (see Appendix B, *Design Thinking Techniques*, p. 196, for context and details).

Defining Design Thinking: User-Centric Thinking

Design Thinking is about putting people first—the people who will use what you're designing, building, and delivering. For this reason, Design Thinking is also called *user-centric* and *human centered* thinking. The CEO of IDEO, Tim Brown, defines Design Thinking as a "human-centered approach to innovation that draws from the designer's toolkit to integrate the needs of people, the possibilities of technology, and the requirements for business success" (Brown, n.d.).

To best understand a user's needs, it is necessary to know them and their mindset, and to understand that user's broader environment, constraints, and ultimate goals. By understanding and empathizing with a user's situation and needs, we can learn the dimensions of their problems and can then design potential solutions.

This broad situational understanding combined with a more narrow or specific user-centric level of empathy is akin to the colloquialisms "walking a mile in their shoes" or "wearing their hat." In the end, observing and really learning what a typical **Day In The Life** of a person comprises helps us understand that person's work, life, and needs.

Approaches to Design Thinking differ in some significant ways (see Figure 2.1), but they all ultimately revolve around getting to know a set of users, defining a problem, ideating and prototyping a potential solution, testing that potential solution, and iterating on it to ultimately arrive at a needs-aligned best fit.

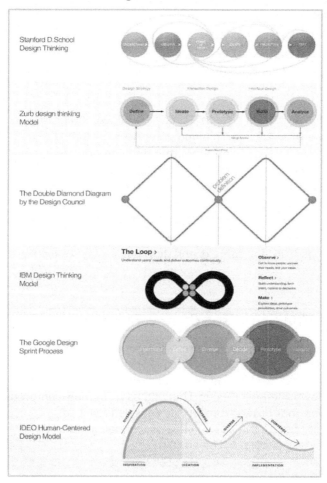

Figure 2.1 Several Design Thinking models in use today (Elmansy, 2018).

In the world of complex Program and Project Management, many of these approaches or models are incomplete. Why? They do not comprise Program or Project Management's end-to-end needs.

Too many Design Thinking models fail to include the notion of Understanding the broader environment as a first step towards understanding users within that environment... or include a final step of Deploying a solution to Users and therefore realizing the value of the entire effort.

Many Design Thinking models conclude with a tested solution in hand but with no regard to deploying that solution (and realizing the value and benefits that such a deployment represents).

So for our purposes here, where we are focused on extending Design Thinking to improve how quickly we can understand the environment and users, define problems, iteratively solve or "solution" them, and deploy those solutions in the context of complex Programs and Projects, we have developed a five step or five component *Design Thinking Model for Program and Project Management* (Figure 2.2).

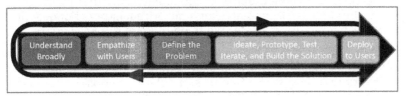

Figure 2.2 Our Design Thinking Model for Program and Project Management.

To apply Design Thinking to improve how quickly we deliver value through transformational programs and projects, it is necessary to overlay our end-to-end Design Thinking model and its five components atop standard Program and Project Management phases as seen in Figure 2.3 (we will cover the basics of Program and Project Management later in Chapter 3 which starts on p. 50). That is, we want to apply the *Understand-Empathize-Define-Solution-Deploy* Design Thinking process to Program and Project Initiation, and Planning, and Mobilizing and Executing, and Controlling and Monitoring, and eventually to Closing and Next Steps. Each phase in a Program or Project demands this Design Thinking perspective so we not only *complete* the work of a Program or Project, but do so more quickly, at less cost and less risk, and at the right level of quality.

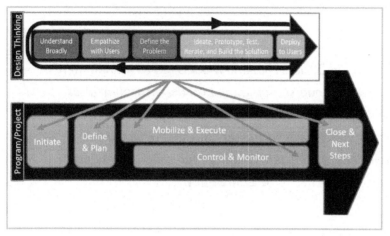

Figure 2.3 Apply our Design Thinking Model to every Program/Project phase.

Understanding Broadly: The Path to Empathy

If Design Thinking is about making progress faster to achieve a desired outcome, it is necessary to understand the broader situation or environment surrounding that outcome. We must **Understand Broadly**.

Doing so means first exploring our user community's broader industry, environment, in-process or pending economic or regulatory changes, and other macro or big-picture matters. We need to learn the answers to questions such as:

- What is the health of the end user community's or organization's industry or landscape (economics, problems, trends)?

- Which regulatory and compliance mandates are top of mind?

- Are there specific industry practices, processes, and quality bars to be considered?

- What are the most relevant external pressures and changes (i.e. competitive pressures, economic changes, or regulatory issues)?

- Where does the organization rank in its industry?

- What differentiates the organization from otherwise similar organizations? How are they different, and why?

Next, we need to learn more about the user's organization itself:

- What is the overall vision of the organization? Who do they aspire to be, and what is the timeframe for that to-be vision?

- What is the general state of the organization from a financial, customer success, work/life balance, and employee morale perspective?

- How is the organization handling external pressures and changes?

- What are the Top 10 organization-specific business or operational pain points and challenges?

- What are the organization's Top 5 strategic business or operational strategies or initiatives?

- With regard to these Top 5 strategies, is the organization protecting rather than **Tossing out Traditional Strategies**? Are they thinking about growth or focused more on protecting a sacred cow? Are they overly concerned about containing costs at the exclusion of the top line? Are they running *from* something rather than *to* something?

- How has the organization's strategy fared lately, and what is changing or could potentially change that would, in turn, affect strategy?

Finally, we need to learn more about the specific Business Unit (BU) or Units with which we will be working:

- How positively is the Business Unit perceived externally and internally?

- What changes in the Business Unit's functional strategies and capabilities are needed?

- How well are current functional capabilities delivered (and how mature is this delivery capability)?

- For any given Program or Project, is there a track record of identifying and rallying around business-specific or operations-specific change drivers?

- To what extent is the Business Unit capable of changing?

- Does the Business Unit's culture (or organization's culture) enable or prohibit change?

- What does "value" mean, and how is value measured?

- How stable is the Business Unit from a leadership and management perspective?

- What do the people working in the Business Unit think about their work, their leaders, their own BU, and their all-up organization?

With all of this broad understanding and context in place, we can then look more deeply into a **Day in the Life** of a specific audience, set of users, or the all-important *individual user*, covered next.

Learning about and Empathizing with Users

Once we understand the big picture, we need to understand a **Day in the Life** of our users and teams for whom our solutions and other outcomes are targeted. Remember that our "users" in this case could be people who will work with the PMO, or our Sponsor, or the team that will help us test, or traditional business system end-users, and others.

Never forget that users with whom we can empathize are everywhere; where there is a problem, there is a user pleading to be heard and understood.

For example, if our users are Program stakeholders, or the staff of the PMO, or members of an Executive Steering Committee, then the underlying problem-to-be-solved could be as diverse as understanding what it means to create a useful Program Charter, or a modular Project Plan, or an effective Executive Communications slide deck.

Methods and approaches for learning about our users, regardless of who they are or the roles they hold, might include:

- Getting to know users at different sites, offices, warehouses, and factories through interviews, observation, **Day in the Life** analysis, and similar real-time *discovery* techniques. To really learn who they are and what's important, invite people to tell the **Stories** that best illuminate their pain and needs.

- Using lightweight Surveys and similar asynchronous *discovery* tools, keeping in mind that current research suggests sample sizes as small as 5 can provide solid insight (Gay, 2019); sample sizes beyond 5 respondents yield markedly diminishing returns.

- Creating a matrix of user **Personas** (or *types* of users) to help us organize how and who to include in specific interviews, surveys, and so on.

- Talking with users about the tools that they currently use (PMO team members will already use certain tools for tracking milestones, publishing meeting minutes, creating and maintaining Project Plans, and reporting status); consider how effective these are and what can or should be reused.

- Learning how users actually interact with their current tools and solutions (ask them to perform for you a lightweight or hands-on **Demonstration** of their current tool and process).

- Asking open-ended questions and other questioning techniques (covered throughout Chapter 5, *Communications*, p. 74).

- **Shadowing** a user or set of users to learn what a day in the life looks like, especially if such an exercise can be repeated several times to identify the 80-90% of tasks that are consistent day-to-day and the 10-20% of tasks that are less frequently executed.

- Distilling our learnings and observations into **Customer Journey Maps** to help us understand what they use today, how they use it, current benefits and shortcomings, and what is accomplished at each step. Such a map helps us better understand how a user interacts with and feels about their work before, during, and after the work is completed.

Remember that these **Design Thinking** techniques are outlined further in Appendix B, *Design Thinking Techniques*. Once we understand our users (knowing that "understanding" is never really complete but rather a work in progress), we can turn our attention to defining their current challenges and problems.

Defining Challenges and Problems

A common mistake in many "solutioning" exercises is too quickly jumping into creating solutions without really understanding the problem. The Design Thinking process forces us to consider the problem, arrive at some level of consensus about the problem, and ultimately *create a problem statement* which we can then set about solving.

> *It's this notion of ever-increasing clarity around problem definition, and the confirmation that we are solving (or on the path to solving) the right problem, that gives Design Thinking much of its power.*

Steps to defining and documenting the problem to be solved include:

- Dusting off the various Charters, Vision Statements, and Missions Statements related to our Program or Project and (assuming they're still accurate), using these artifacts as a foundation and set of boundaries describing the big picture

- Bringing together what we learned through the Understand Broadly and Empathize with Users components of our *Design Thinking Model for Program and Project Management*

- Pulling out user direct quotes, verbatims, **Stories**, and other feedback, and documenting user challenges and pain points

- Mapping the challenges and pain points back to user **Personas** or roles and specific **Customer Journey Maps**

- Considering how our users or audiences are varied in terms of overall organizational culture and team or workplace climate

- Using techniques such as the **Five Why's** to learn more and then refine what we know into a discreet Problem Statement

- Forcing ourselves to consider these challenges and pain points more broadly as we up-level our *thinking* and our Problem Statement in search of high-order themes; it is here that we need to push ourselves and our teams to go beyond the obvious

- Distilling what we know about the 80-90% **Day in the Life** common use cases and 10-20% unique or **Edge Cases**, and then applying that Edge Case insight into the broader thinking necessary to reframe the challenges and pain points to update our Problem Statement

Though we may still have many questions, at this point we should have consensus around an *initial* Problem Statement and higher-order themes, recognizing that we will continue to learn and refine as we go.

Iteratively Solutioning for Usability

After initial problem definition (where complex problems are indeed still ambiguous), the next step or component of Design Thinking is solution-oriented. We often break out this iterative work into distinct tasks or sub-components. These sub-components all work together and inform one another, creating an exploratory process for discovery and learning (Brown, 2019) through iterative **Feedback Loops**. Feedback helps us further refine and solve the right problem to build the right solution.

We like to call this collection of Design Thinking tasks or sub-components **Solutioning**, where the goal is to achieve the right level of usability and detail before we finally create the initial solution to be deployed to users (understanding that even then, post-deployment, this imperfect initial solution will still go through **Iterations** of refinement). These tasks or sub-components are outlined next.

Ideating or Brainstorming

Often simply called **Brainstorming** (which is actually just one of several ideating techniques), the work of ideating is to think through and around a problem broadly. Effective ideating demands a **Design Mindset**.

Ideation is the search for a nugget of a solution.

We are also seeking to corroborate and refine (and possibly re-define) our notion of the problem itself. No idea is a bad idea when we are brainstorming, especially given the complexity of business and organizational transformations, operational transformations, and other complex undertakings.

Complete solutions are highly improbable during ideation. Thus, ideas that yield even a partial solution are especially welcome; partial and potential solutions are typically the best we can do in the short term. But these partial and potential ideas and solutions give us our starting point. And it's these early ideas spawned through ideation and brainstorming that give us an anchor for our earliest prototyping and building efforts (again, refer to Appendix B, *Design Thinking Techniques*, starting on page 196 for more information and other techniques).

- What can we do to promote a **Design Mindset** where our people are solution-focused rather than problem-focused?

- Are we forcing deep thinking through the use **Mind Mapping** and other techniques to organize and explore our ideas?

- Are we performing **Premortems** and similar "thinking ahead" exercises? Are we considering where failures or issues lie over the horizon, and creating *obstacle lists* for teams to consider?

- Are we learning from the enduring words shared in **Cobb's Paradox** (1995) and matrix/survey tool? Are we using this as a fundamental user-centric Ideation tool? For objective ideation and assessment, are there other Survey tools we should employ to gather diverse user assessments and perspectives?

- Are we really prepared to think differently and deeply? For example, instead of trying to answer a question or think about a really difficult problem head-on through brainstorming, we might need to reverse the question or problem and have the team think about what would make the problem *worse*. This **Reverse Brainstorming** technique is useful in that afterwards the team can "flip" their thinking and therefore work through answering the original question or problem.

- Ideating eventually benefits from and is refined by **Feedback** gained through rapid prototyping, testing, and iterating. What are we doing to instrument that feedback?

Having a hard time getting people in the **Design Mindset** to think and create solutions? Consider using Legos® as ice breakers and to help teams think creatively prior to attempting to brainstorm a "real" issue. Give each team member a bag with 50 random pieces and verbal instructions to literally build a bridge with another person; this dual-purpose exercise naturally breaks down walls, promotes or yields **Collaboration**, develops relationships, and ultimately drives a lightweight version of **Co-Innovation**.

Prototyping

The notion of prototyping is two-fold. First, we want to practice "Building to Think" rather than thinking and planning and thinking before finally trying to build something. The idea is that we have much to learn given the ambiguity we naturally face, so the trade-off in building early is well worth the *throw-away* work associated with many failed prototyping attempts. Why? Because prototyping is about failing early and cheaply (though it may be more accurate to say "learning early and cheaply").

Second, we need to ensure we are truly learning and failing *quickly*; realizing improved time-to-value is a speed play after all. The faster we fail and learn, the faster we can incorporate these learnings back into a new iteration of the prototype... or course-correct and create a completely new set of options, including an entirely new prototype.

> *Prototyping serves many purposes; we're learning, we're course-correcting, we're teasing out new options, and we're further informing our understanding of the environment, our users, their problems, and the nature of a potential solution.*

Prototyping is therefore the first source of our **Feedback Loops**, in this case out of solutioning and back into the earlier steps of Design Thinking. Consider the following prototyping methods:

- Get started by actually *doing* something; start building to help you think more deeply.

- Capture and record all the Use Cases or user scenarios, both typical and **Edge Cases**. Then pick the 10 most important.

- Reserve a big conference room that facilitates creating and working through the 10 most important Use Cases. Set some basic ground rules and create an atmosphere of design and collaboration.

- Draw, draw, draw... Create **Mind Maps** and **Storyboards** and timelines and customer journeys and organizational structures...

- Sketch out or whiteboard a solution's data flows, work-flows, interfaces, and so on, whiteboarding **Personas** and team connections along the way.

- Whiteboard or wire-frame user interfaces or deliverables; create non-functioning "illustrations" and other visuals using Microsoft PowerPoint, Adobe Photoshop, or a developer toolset.

- Whiteboard to promote **Modular Thinking and Building**; review existing **Standard Templates** and create high-level mock project plan *modules* or high-level Tables of Content for key deliverables, so you can get a feel for what is needed and how to logically organize the content.

- Animate static figures and pictures to show step-wise movement or other changes; Microsoft PowerPoint is still one of the easiest and most lightweight tools for quickly **Mocking Up**, animating, and quickly iterating on designs, use cases, and **Storyboards**.

- **Demonstrate** these whiteboard drawings, visuals, and other mock-ups to real users *early* to obtain their feedback around usability, logical organization, completeness, and overall consumability. Is the team on the right track?

Testing

Testing is the second and most critical **Feedback Loop** of Design Thinking Solutioning. Through testing, we will learn to what extent our prototype is on the right track. We will see opportunities to improve the prototype. And we will identify gaps in the prototype's capabilities or functionality, which will take us back to considering what we know and broadly understand, how we might empathize differently, and how we might change our notion of the Problem Statement(s).

Build to Think and Test to Learn.

To help us test and learn well, consider the following:

- Embrace several types of lightweight and user-centric testing. Our initial tests should allow us to move quickly through a "test-iterate-ideate-prototype and test again" cycle.

- As our prototype begins to evolve into more of a legitimate solution, our testing should evolve as well to help us validate relevant **Edge Cases** and work through more detailed use cases or user scenarios. We will eventually need to perform end-to-end process tests, performance tests, scalability and smoke tests, integration tests, user acceptance tests, and other tests intended to help us learn, iterate, and confirm.

- After what could very well be many iterations working through our prototype and building a solution, we will ultimately need to run *User Acceptance Testing* to give our users an opportunity to work through real-world scenarios and provide even more reality-grounded feedback.

- We may need to employ other specific types of testing to address or accommodate specific situations; think ahead to identify how to make those specific situations *testable*.

- Similarly, we will need to focus our testing around specific groups of users, audiences, or **Personas**; think through and identify early the test personas or types of users we will need for testing, so we can align the right people, schedules, and expectations. Consider their **Customer Journey Maps**.

Above all, remember to stay nimble! We need to work responsibly through testing, but we need to do so in a way that helps us learn fast and make progress. Keep overhead and overall governance lightweight enough to help us arrive at the place where we iterate, test, and iterate again until we finally build our preliminary solution, covered next.

Iterating and Building

Arguably the most powerful aspect of Design Thinking lies in the power of iterating to eventually build a solution. As needed, bake testing learnings into another iteration of ideating, prototyping, and testing.

It's in the repetition of iterating, re-testing, and eventually building that we fine-tune our thinking, our understanding of the problem, and ultimately the fit of our solution.

Iterating as a process for building also allows us to:

- Clean up and clarify our user's requirements
- Identify new and important **Edge Cases** previously missed
- Introduce both back-end (IT) and front-end (business or operations) design changes while such changes are still relatively easy to make

- Investigate and iterate on *usability* early on; for example, we should consider **Inclusive or Sensitive Design** implications as we think through new user communities and their needs

- Quickly create a **Minimum Viable Product** (MVP or minimal solution) that can actually deliver a level of functionality or other value to users while still evolving—through additional iterations—to become the full-fledged solution envisioned in the first place

Deploying the Solution to Users

The notion of actually deploying a solution (after we have understood, empathized, ideated, designed, prototyped, tested, iterated upon, and built) is absent in many Design Thinking models.

---

*Benefits realization in the form of using the solution is our goal, so we need to give special attention to the final step in the model: How we **deploy** to users.*

In our world of large-scale Program and Project Management, deployment itself can be incredibly complex. It therefore demands its own round of Design Thinking. For starters, solution deployments need to be planned. Important questions to be answered include:

- What kind of variety is represented by the solution's end-user community in terms of audiences, **Personas**, teams, physical locations, time zones, languages, culture, and work climate?

- How mature or experienced is the end-user community? How many different user communities are there?

- Is there an early adopter subset of each user community naturally or otherwise well positioned to accept the solution first (such as those most in tune with the organization's future vision, or willing to take risks and experiment, or willing to do the hard work of communicating and iterating in a solution's early days)?

- Is the desire to learn and adopt something new present in the end-user community (or a subset of the community)?

- Conversely, is there resistance to change that still needs to be addressed?

- How and when (using what kinds of tools) will end users be trained just-in-time before deployment?

- What is the timing between the final round of solution testing and the first round of solution deployments?

- Can we perform a pilot deployment to a small number of users (to learn even more than we did during prototyping and testing) prior to rolling out the solution more broadly?

- Should the solution be rolled out in one giant *big bang* or in waves or rings or phases to best accommodate the user community? Are there **Time Pacing** constraints to consider?

- How would a phased deployment affect other systems or processes that may need to be kept in sync until the solution is fully deployed to all users?

- Are there Disaster Recovery or Business Continuity considerations that need to be planned for, coordinated, and accommodated while the solution is being deployed?

- Are there special "black-out periods" that need to be avoided, such as month-end financial closing, key Program or Project milestones dates, peak Project Team or end user vacation periods, seasonal peaks such as Black Friday or Cyber Monday, deployments of other competing or conflicting changes within the user community, and so on?

- Are there any financial or other constraints that could affect Program or Project funding for deployments after a given timeframe (or under other circumstances)? Do we therefore need to change or otherwise **Align our deployment Strategy to specific Time Horizons**?

- Do we have dependencies between our deployment and current legacy systems or third-party systems related to upgrades, end of life, or in-flight implementations that could affect us from a resourcing or financial or other perspective?

- How will we capture, synthesize, and potentially incorporate inevitable **Silent Design** feedback from our users?

We find that working backwards from a target final deployment date helps inform which of these deployment considerations are show-stoppers, which need more clarity, and which can be accommodated. We then need to "build to think" a prototype roll-out schedule and plan, sharing it early and iterating on it quickly as the team pokes holes in the plan and makes others observations. Unsurprisingly, the least risky deployment plans include **Piloting** the solution to a subset of users before rolling it out more broadly.

Prior to executing the Deployment Plan, we need to think through how we are going to support our users during the transition from the old to the new. Consider the following:

- Do we have the necessary support people, and do those people have the bandwidth, skills, qualifications, and tools necessary to support users well?

- Do we have the ability to capture, monitor, and measure issues and learnings along the way, including actual user engagement and **User Engagement Metrics** including user adoption?

Once we are executing the plan and in the midst of solution deployments, we need to follow Design Thinking precepts related to learning and iterating. However, fight the urge to use our in-flight learnings to course correct then and there! Instead, we need to remain focused first and foremost on actually delivering something of value, recognizing that the road to perfection never ends. Our mantra needs to be "Deploy to realize Value today, and capture Learnings to increase that Value tomorrow."

Record in our Knowledge Management system

(Lessons Learned register) what we learn from our

users about a Solution along the way to help us

improve on that Solution after it has been deployed.

A Sampling of Design Thinking Techniques

Beyond the "building to think" and prototyping and testing and iterating practices outlined so far, we will be employing more than **70 Design Thinking** techniques, strategies, tools, and methods as we work our way through the book. Some of the Design Thinking techniques we will apply to Program and Project Management include the following:

Note that more than 70 Design Thinking techniques are outlined in Appendix B, *Design Thinking Techniques*, starting on p. 196.

- **Aligning Strategy to Time Horizons.** We need to think about the today, the short-term, the mid-term, and the long-term, recognizing that our long-term vision must be prioritized to be realized.

- **Drawing on Adjacent Spaces.** As we change anything in our Program or Project, consider how we can incrementally ease into the "white space" or conceptual adjacent space surrounding our current processes, methods, tools, and so on, with the idea that such change is more easily adopted or consumed because it is similar to what is currently in place.

- **Regenerating through Combining.** Consider how we can combine the old with the new in a modular way, the outcome of which is naturally "less new" and therefore more consumable.

- **Applying the Inverse Power Law.** Introduce a high number of little changes, a fewer number of medium changes, and only a very few number of major changes (just as we observe in biology and nature, i.e. earthquake frequencies or ecosystem changes).

- **Applying Inclusive (or Sensitive) Design.** Consider the abilities of a user community in the context of its culture, values, lifestyle, and preferences; allow this knowledge to influence with whom we empathize and how and what we design and deliver.

- **Practicing Divergent Thinking.** Rather than trying to find the "right" answer to a problem, challenge current thinking (or ideas or designs) as a way to explore the surrounding situation.

- **Engaging in Co-Innovation.** Develop and iterate on solutions and artifacts together with partners, team members, and users in real-time side-by-side to speed up solutioning and testing.

- **Scaling for Effectiveness.** Consider the best way to scale the work or effort in front of you, using either a highly repeatable replication or *franchise* approach or an intentionally varied or *boutique* approach.

- **Using Premortems.** Think ahead as to what might fail and then build mitigations or user involvement to avoid those failures.

- **Considering Time Pacing.** Solutions exhibit rhythms in use. Understanding the peaks and valleys of a solution's utilization helps thoughtfully structure staffing and deployment changes and create the most effective/least impactful rollout strategies.

While several of these techniques are pretty common, others might be quite foreign to you. We will walk through *and apply* these and many other Design Thinking techniques and strategies throughout the book.

Guiding Principles for User-Centric Thinking

To help facilitate user-centric or empathetic thinking, consider using or adapting the following Guiding Principles:

- Understand broadly to empathize; know the history and the "Why" behind this history.

- Not all users are the same, and not all problems affect a single user in the same way.

- Meet your users where they are, and then bring them along.

- Deliver early and iterate quickly with a core group of users.

- "Build to Think" rather than "Think to Build" until it becomes necessary to think deeply again.

- The feedback from as few as five users has been shown to illuminate 90% of a team's requirements; focus on working with the best five.

- Think and design deeply so your users can do what they need to do *without* thinking deeply.

- Prototype to test assumptions and refine the Problem Statement.

- Fail and learn *fast* to fail and learn *cheaply*.

Chapter Summary

In our second chapter, we defined Design Thinking and explored a model for thinking about and applying Design Thinking to Program and Project Management. This model extends typical Design Thinking models on the front end and back end. On the front end, we have included the need to Understand (the environment) Broadly. To realize the value of our work, on the back end we have included the need to Deploy (our solution) to Users. We walked through each of the five steps or components of the model (Understand, Empathize, Define the Problem, Solution the Problem, and Deploy the Solution), concluding with a number of sample Design Thinking techniques we will employ on our Program and Project journey.

All of the Design Thinking techniques explored here and elsewhere are outlined in Appendix B, *Design Thinking Techniques*, starting on p. 196.

Chapter Case Study

Falcon Advanced Shipping and Transport's business leads have heard you discuss your thoughts around the benefits of Design Thinking for Program and Project Management, and they want to know more. One of the leads has organized a meeting to explore your thinking, and they've asked you to set the stage by expanding on a short list of questions.

Chapter 2: Questions

1. What are the five steps or five components of the *Design Thinking Model for Program and Project Management*?
2. Why was the fifth and final step or component added to the *Design Thinking Model for Program and Project Management*?
3. What aspects or phases of traditional Program and Project Management should be informed or influenced by Design Thinking?
4. What does "Understanding Broadly" mean in the context of learning or empathizing?
5. What does "Building to Think" mean with regards to prototyping?

See Appendix A starting on p. 187 for Case Study answers.

Chapter 3

Program & Project Management Basics

Good Program and Project Management or P&PM sets the stage for successful delivery of a service, capability, or outcome. While P&PM is mature given its time-tested and industry-neutral processes, the premise of this book assumes we can deliver P&PM more effectively and a Program's or Project's outcomes more quickly. This chapter sets the stage for understanding Program and Project Management basics so we in turn can explore what it means to apply Design Thinking to its phases and processes.

Program and Project Management: Delivering Value

Overseeing a Program or Project comprises managing a great number of tasks, people, conflicting timelines, and competing priorities. From understanding and working effectively within a project's unique cultural and social environment to navigating political factors, working through varying levels of interpersonal and business skills, and more, P&PM presents tough challenges for even the most seasoned Program or Project Management professionals. But the simple and universal truth is that a Program or Project must deliver its intended value to make all this time and effort worthwhile; there is no second place. *It is the time and effort required to deliver this value,* if indeed it is ever delivered, that is at stake. Otherwise, it would have been smarter to forgo the Program or Project altogether, preserving the time and effort for other endeavors.

Program Management Basics: Navigating the Strategic

As we know, Program Management differs from Project Management. Programs are the large-scale and typically long-term endeavors that organizations purse to effect fundamental change. Programs act as an umbrella covering a collection of related Component Projects that, together, work to deliver the intended fundamental change.

But there is more than size and scope differences at stake. Given their focus on effecting fundamental change, Programs are by definition more strategic than their Project counterparts.

> *Think of Programs as strategic umbrellas focused on broad-based value and benefits realization, and Projects as tactical efforts intended to deliver a specific set of capabilities or value.*

Programs necessitate big-picture thinking and careful resource alignment to achieve broad organizational objectives. How a Program is structured, and how its Component Projects and dependencies are managed to achieve benefits (that would otherwise be unrealized if these underlying projects were managed in a stand-alone fashion) are key to realizing these broader organizational objectives (PgMP Handbook, 2019).

More art than science, managing a Program amounts to managing the following strategic Program-level processes and their sub-components:

- **Strategy Management**
    - Program Charter
    - Organizational strategy & business case

- Program roadmap, including how the Program fits into the organization's broader portfolio of Programs and other initiatives

- **Benefits Management**

  - Benefits realization plan

  - Benefits transition and sustainment plan

- **Stakeholder Engagement and Expectations Management**

  - Engagement and expectations management plans and artifacts including the **Stakeholder Map** and register, and the stakeholder analysis worksheet

  - Processes for keeping stakeholders engaged

  - Processes for managing stakeholder expectations

  - Techniques for measuring Program/Project health

- **Program Life Cycle Management**

  - Program life cycle phases, including Definition (Initiating & Planning), Delivery (Executing & Monitoring), and Closure (Transition & Closing)

  - Key Program-level operations processes, including partner collaboration and communications management, lessons learned, retrospective management, and others

- **Program Governance**

  - Program governance plan

  - Structure and makeup of the various governance bodies

  - Governance roles and responsibilities matrix

  - Governance communications plan, including the cadence for meetings, scheduled stage gates and approval processes, and decision-making and escalation processes

Through all of this, a Program Manager is also managing several Project Managers who are delivering their respective Projects, covered next.

Project Management Basics: Executing the Tactical

If Program Management is an art, Project Management is more akin to science; it is prescriptive, process and task oriented, and well understood. Managing projects equates to managing a set of iterative processes for initiating the work, planning and doing the work, and then checking the work to confirm quality (Anderson, Nilson, et al, 2009):

- **Projects are bound by the triple constraints** or *Iron Triangle* of scope, time, and cost. Successful projects deliver precisely what has been contracted while negotiating changes in the constraints; a change in one constraint impacts the remaining constraints. For example, an increase in scope will almost always change the cost or schedule or both.

- **Projects compete with one another** for the limited organizational resources (i.e. people, time, and budgets) necessary to complete a specified body of work intended to achieve a specific set of results or outcomes.

- **Projects are temporary** rather than ongoing operational endeavors and thus come to a halt for any number of reasons.

Healthy projects naturally wind down at some point, but less healthy projects may end prematurely due to a lack of sponsorship interest, loss of funding or key personnel, changes in prioritization, mis-managed resources, unclear requirements, poorly managed scope changes, an inability to fund needed changes, inadequate or ineffective leadership, poor project planning and project execution practices, mishandled communications, changes in executive or end-user buy-in, lack of consensus regarding the project's expected outcomes or benefits realization, and other such matters.

Projects require sound task management, process diligence, active leadership, and outstanding governance. In the end, though, experience and research alike demonstrate that good project management hinges on staffing projects with excellent Project Managers.

What is an excellent Project Manager? In our experience, the most effective project managers balance communications and task management skills with effective situational leadership, people skills, personal courage, an ability to successfully juggle competing priorities, and political deftness. Because this combination of skills and attributes is difficult to find in a single individual, "poor project management" has long been cited as one of the top culprits behind failed projects (Cobb, 1995). Look to the Project Management Institute's (2017) guidance for additional insight.

The sixth edition of "A Guide to the Project Management Body of Knowledge" (or the PMBOK® Guide), published by the Project Management Institute in 2017, is our preferred source for understanding Project Management and to a lesser extent Program Management.

Program and Project Management Phases

Project Management tasks and processes are organized into a number of step-wise or time-oriented phases. The Project Management Institute (2017) calls these *process groups* (or collections of processes related to one another). We adapted and slightly modified the Project Management Institute's phases to meet our needs here (Figure 3.1).

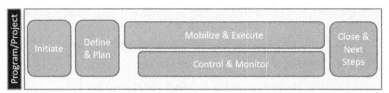

Figure 3.1 The five Design Thinking-influenced Phases of P&PM.

Specifically, our modified and broader interpretation accommodates Design Thinking while spanning both Program and Project Management:

- **Initiate.** Includes the pre-planning and mobilization processes that commence the project, including coming to an agreement as to project scope, what is out of scope, and other foundational realities.

- **Define and Plan.** Includes processes that identify what actually needs to be accomplished, broken down into achievable tasks and milestones. Sometimes this is referred to as blueprinting or discovery. The processes in this planning process group are used to refine and detail the objectives set out during the initiating phase, including the specific tasks and milestones necessary to achieve those objectives.

- **Mobilize and Execute.** Includes processes that support the "real work" of completing the project's specific tasks. These include pulling together the resources required to fulfill the Project Management Plan.

- **Control and Monitor.** Includes processes that keep the project on track including overall project scope, cost, and quality, and to monitor the project's progress (such as determining which tasks are running ahead of plan, which tasks are running behind, and which tasks require additional support or corrective action).

- **Close and Next Steps.** Includes processes that effectively conclude the project; the closing process group includes processes that describe formal acceptance of the overall project's outcomes and what it means to bring the project to a successful conclusion.

While not a phase in its own right, a sixth critically important component to Program and Project Management lies in the following:

- **Integration.** Includes executing and managing the processes, people, and knowledge spanning a Program or Project, all of which must come together to realize value; coordinating and connecting the overall work among and between Component Projects or other workstreams; making smart or necessary trade-offs in the name of Program benefits realization; understanding and connecting dependencies between Component Projects and Projects or dependencies outside of a Program; and ultimately delivering a solution that solves the right problem(s).

Integration management starts with the Initiate phase and continues through the Close and Next Steps phase. To simplify, though, we view Integration as an important part of Program and Project *Execution*.

All of these phases are standard across various project implementation methodologies regardless of industry or geography or the type of Program or Project. In subsequent chapters, we will look at these phases in greater detail as we apply Design Thinking where it can be most impactful. In the remainder of this chapter, however, each phase is briefly explored to give us a shared understanding of how most of the world naturally views and works through these standard phases.

The Initiate Phase

The Initiate Phase, based generally on the Project Management Institute's (2017) Initiating process group, formally authorizes a new Program or Project. Key activities must be completed, such as:

- Identifying and aligning with the Sponsor, who initiates the Program or Project and then regularly meets with the business/operations team and the PMO leadership team to reinforce the vision, address escalations and strategic matters, and make tough decisions

- Publishing the Charter which formalizes the business/operational need for the Program or Project and links the two together

- Identifying key roles and responsibilities, high-level timelines, and conditions of satisfaction

- Creating a preliminary scope statement including a high-level work definition and statement of work, enterprise/organizational information, preliminary plans, requirements, and high-level expected outcomes and deliverables

- Developing a preliminary budget to begin positioning the overall body of work within the organization's broader portfolio of Programs and Projects

- Commencing the work of securing key resources

The Define and Plan Phase

The Project Management Institute (2017) explains that the Planning process group refines project objectives and iterates on other work created when the effort is initiated. For our purposes, we are also defining and refining our understanding of the Program or Project's underlying purpose, the problems to be solved, how those problems will be solved, and more. Our Define and Plan Phase finalizes the scope, standards, and boundaries of a Program or Project and documents key constraints, dates, dependencies, and other considerations.

Importantly, critical Program and Project Management plans are formulated at this time. These plans come together to create our master plan or *playbook* for delivering the Program or Project. As we have mentioned elsewhere, these plans include our overall Program Management Plan, Governance Plan, Benefits Realization Plan, Quality Plan, Communications Plan, and Stakeholder Engagement Plan.

Many of these planning items can surely be worked on earlier in the Initiate phase, and indeed we *want* to iterate and evolve our understanding early on. Just be aware that planning and iterating on too much too early will yield a certain amount of *throw-away* or duplicated effort in terms of work products, plans, and so on. The benefits of understanding earlier-than-later is almost always worth the early-on investment in time, however, as we seek to accelerate from the Initiate phase to the Define and Plan phase. Early understanding makes it more likely we will avoid even *more* rework later, when schedules are difficult to alter and stakeholder expectations are more deeply cemented.

The Mobilize and Execute Phase

Once planning is largely completed, we need to mobilize our resources and commence delivering the work of the Program or Project, including:

- Onboarding remaining core team members as well as new ones

- Holding any final *discovery* or *solutioning* workshops needed for additional clarity (understanding that clarity in some areas will necessarily evolve over time)

- Creating and managing the development of work products and other deliverables as identified in the scope of work

- Reviewing and prioritizing requested changes to the scope of work

- Obtaining sign-offs for, and then planning and implementing, approved changes requests

- Course-correcting as necessary to ensure the Program's or Project's work products and other outcomes meet agreed-upon standards, timelines, and budgets

- Proactively updating the risk management plan as new risks are identified or realized

- Reactively addressing project issues (that is, *realized risks*)

- Performing the bulk of Integration Management or managing the integration of processes, knowledge, and people, acknowledging that this work of integrating and connecting necessarily spans the entire Program or Project lifecycle.

Integration management requires that a Program or Project Manager identify, define, combine, unify, and coordinate all of the various processes and project management activities (Project Management Institute, 2017, p. 69). It is through this insight that the Manager can make smarter resource allocation decisions, balance competing demands, consider alternative approaches, fine-tune processes, and ultimately better manage the myriad of external and inter-dependencies.

More broadly, managing project execution means gathering information describing what, how, and when the work has been performed, managing late work, working ahead of schedule when possible, tracking overall schedule variations, and mapping those variations, other changes, and new or updated dependencies back to key milestones and the overall timeline.

During execution, it is critical to track how changes in the work affect the Program's and Project's *critical path*, or the string of tasks that must be completed for the overall body of work to conclude on time and on budget at the agreed-upon level of quality.

The Control and Monitor Phase

Once the Program or Project is underway, it is necessary to monitor and control and govern its delivery. Our goal is to ensure that our ongoing work is directionally aligned, and that our deliverables and work products are delivered according to the scope of work (presumably therefore meeting stakeholder expectations). Called governance or oversight, this Control and Monitor phase comprises a combination of real-time, weekly, and monthly monitoring and controlling. Key activities include:

- Tracking and managing work scope (plus or minus approved changes)

- Ensuring budgets and costs are on plan

- Validating work product quality

- Tracking variances to plan

- Communicating those variances, along with status and pending decisions, with the appropriate team members and stakeholders

Project variances in scope, schedule, cost, resourcing, and more are inevitable. Many of these deviations can be addressed by the PMO or the local leadership team. However, significant and unresolvable issues must be escalated to the appropriate governance body for speedy resolution. Such escalation is not only expected but appropriate and healthy under the right circumstances.

Do not be afraid to escalate problems *fast and high* to executive decision-makers. In our experience, executive decision-makers expect to be called into play to act as tiebreakers and to make difficult decisions. Use them sooner rather than later.

Monitoring and controlling drives the need for a number of governance bodies required for Program or Project success. Governance bodies range from the PMO itself to architecture and technology review boards, to multi-level Steering Committees and other executive boards, to Change Review boards and special-purpose boards.

Interestingly, the reason for a significant number of failed Programs and Projects can be traced back to failing to engage the proper governance body early enough to make hard decisions.

*Never allow delayed decisions to rob you of the
ability to course correct and finish.*

The Close and Next Steps Phase

The Project Management Institute (2017) tells us that the Closing process group includes processes executed to formally wind down and ultimately terminate or "close" all of the activities outlined in the project plan and scope of work. Said another way, executing the processes that formally close open activities brings about formal closure of the project. For our Design Thinking purposes, particularly with regard to Programs, we have extended Closing to also include **Next Step Thinking**. Doing so allows us to consider how we can capitalize upon what we have already built and how we might further leverage the team that built it, all in the name of "next steps."

The most important thing to keep in mind is that the successful release of any final *work products* on a project schedule does not close a Program or Project; closing needs to be made official through stakeholder agreement that the scope of work has indeed been delivered. Closing a Program is a bit more work than closing a Project, too, as it includes:

- Validating that the strategy has been achieved (or that the strategy is still in progress through other work incorporated in another Program or portfolio of Projects... if that was the plan)

- Validating that the Program's benefits have been achieved (or again, are in progress as agreed)

- Ensuring final communications are shared

How we apply Design Thinking to these important steps around confirming delivered value, performing closing, and thinking through next steps are detailed in Chapter 12.

Summary

Chapter 3 laid the groundwork for Program and Project Management. We outlined the strategic nature of Programs and the tactical realities of Projects. Then we introduced you to important Program and Project Management concepts and the five phases of every Program or Project: Initiate, Define and Plan, Mobilize and Execute, Control and Monitor, and Close and Next Steps.

We outlined the importance of Integration as a sixth component spanning Execution (acknowledging that the integration of processes, people, and knowledge actually starts in the earliest days of a Program or Project). In subsequent chapters, we will apply Design Thinking within and across this Program and Project Management foundation.

All of the Design Thinking techniques we will apply to P&PM are outlined in Appendix B, *Design Thinking Techniques*, starting on p. 196.

Case Study

FAST has recently stood up the Harmony Program's PMO, and the newly appointed Program Director has asked you to review the team's thinking around its understanding of Program and Project Management.

Chapter 3 Questions

1. Regarding Programs and Projects, which is more strategic, and which is more tactical?

2. According to the PgMP Handbook, what are the five strategic program-level processes or *management* areas with which Program Management is concerned?

3. What are the five phases of Design Thinking-inspired Program and Project Management espoused in this chapter?

4. A key aspect of controlling and monitoring a Program or Project involves potential escalation. When and to whom should significant or unresolvable issues be escalated?

See Appendix A starting on p. 187 for Case Study answers.

Chapter 4

Simple Rules and Guiding Principles

o   *Knowing Ourselves through Simple Rules*
o   *A Sampling of Simple Rules*
o   *Effectively Adapting to Change through Guiding Principles*
o   *Guiding Principles for Creating Simple Rules and Guiding Principles*
o   *Chapter Summary and Case Study*

As we outlined in Chapter 1, *Why Design Thinking?*, Best Practices become stale over time, and Common Practices align more with surviving and status quo than driving transformative change. On the other hand, Simple Rules and Guiding Principles can give our Programs and Projects what they need to evolve and survive over the long-term. To help focus on doing the right things at the right time, we need to establish a set of Simple Rules describing "Who" and "What" and "When," followed by a set of Guiding Principles outlining "How" to think and operate across the Program or Project lifecycle (see Figure 4.1).

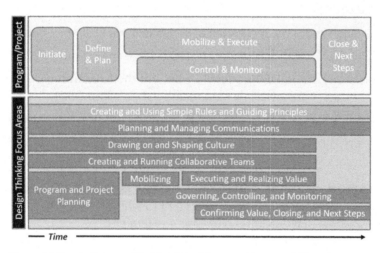

Figure 4.1 Simple Rules and Guiding Principles span the overall lifecycle.

Programs and Projects have a purpose, personality, set of boundaries, time horizons, and a distinctive culture. They are unique. Our Simple Rules and Guiding Principles help work through all of this uniqueness; they codify *ambiguity and complexity* to help us know ourselves and make smarter and faster decisions.

Simple Rules and Guiding Principles provide the guardrails to Programs and Projects, enabling consistency in execution, decisions, and priorities.

Outlining these Simple Rules and Guiding Principles by which to operate is the focus of Chapter 4.

Knowing Ourselves through Simple Rules

Simple Rules are helpful to define "who we are" as a Program or Project, and to align our goals with the perspective or means to achieve those goals. We use Simple Rules at any level of an organization, from a Program down to Component Projects, workstreams, function-specific teams, and virtual teams. Simple Rules could therefore apply to the Program itself, PMO, the Solution Development Team, the Solution Test Team, the Integration Team, the Data Management Team, the Security Team, and others. These Rules may include:

- What we value and their priorities
- When to proceed
- When to pause
- Who plays what role
- What we do & don't do
- What we do to measure our effectiveness
- What our outputs look like
- What we do to drive and measure those outputs
- What we look like externally
- When we make exceptions

Creating our Simple Rules

Simple Rules are best created in **Brainstorming** or **Hackathon** settings with the core team seeking to know itself, walking through the bulleted questions above. This is not a top-down or solo endeavor.

The exercise of creating Simple Rules needs to be performed by the team who will execute and live by those Simple Rules.

It is easy and normal to initially uncover thirty or more Simple Rules. Before the Simple Rules-focused brainstorming session or workshop concludes, however, our goal is to generally organize these Rules into higher-level themes so we can reduce the number of Rules to 10 or so.

With our first set of 10 Simple Rules in our pocket, we should then begin executing against those rules ("building to think"), refining the Rules over several weeks, and ideally identifying maybe six or fewer Simple Rules by which to execute.

We should also think through what it means to change those Rules over time. Course correcting is normal as organizations and teams evolve through phases of a Program or Project. Such changes within function-specific teams probably would not occur more than once in a large Program or Project, though. The more task-focused the team, generally the more static the Simple Rules.

Working through Bottlenecks

Beyond helping us figure out Who we are, When we Operate, and What we represent, Simple Rules are intended to provide a team guidance around what they must do to handle bottlenecks.

Simple Rules help us work through bottlenecks more effectively, leading to greater velocity.

Simple Rules give us what we need to make decisions more quickly. For example, if as a Program we value prototyping to learn and iterating on those prototypes to fine-tune our learning, then heavy-handed governance or a thinly staffed prototyping team would represent bottlenecks or impediments to achieving our outcomes. Similarly, if we run into a funding or budgeting bottleneck, a set of Simple Rules can help us react quickly and in alignment with our core beliefs or operating principles.

A Sampling of Simple Rules

In this section, we explore the Simple Rules employed by a number of real-world organizations. The idea here is to create Simple Rules that help us push through potential roadblocks or other bottlenecks which would otherwise result in wasteful detours and slow-downs.

A Popular Rock Band

To get us accustomed to developing Simple Rules, let's take a look at a whimsical but very real example of Simple Rules in action—a set of Rules developed by the rock band Coldplay. The band sat down in its early days and drew up a list of Simple Rules to help document and drive a consistent artistic process and set of musical outcomes. In *their* words:

1. Albums must be no longer than 42 minutes or 9 tracks.
2. Production must be amazing, rich but with space; not overlayered, less tracks, more quality, groove, and swing. Drums and rhythm are the most crucial thing to concentrate on.
3. Computers are instruments, not recording aids.
4. Imagery must be classic, colourful, and different...
5. Make sure videos and pictures are great before setting Release Date, and highly original.
6. Always keep mystery. Not many interviews.
7. Groove and swing rhythms and sounds must always be original as possible...
8. Promo/review copies to be on vinyl. Stops copying problem, sounds and looks better.
9. Jaqueline Sabriado, ns p cc, face forward.

10. Think about what to do with charity account. Set up something small but really enabling and constructive.

While 10 rules is more than the recommended six, through these Simple Rules the band has remained remarkably consistent in terms of sound, outputs, and specific audience appeal, all while maintaining a singular sense of self and a high level of creativity.

A Large Dental Supply Company

A large Dental Supply company developed a set of Simple Rules to help it prioritize which potential customers (dentists) to pursue. After assessing their own customer database, they found that 10% of their current dental customers accounted for more than half their revenue. Their Simple Rules amounted to identifying common characteristics that would help them grow this base of highly profitable customers:

- We will only target dentists who own their own practice.

- The ideal age of our target dentist is 35-55.

- Every dentist we target should be able to commit to $10,000 in products annually.

- The ideal dentist is currently burdened with less than 5% financing and thus have bandwidth to work with us.

- The ideal dentist has attended our company-specific training program.

After a month of practicing these Rules, they determined that the first Rule did not really matter much, and the ability to commit to $5000 rather than $10,000 was nearly identical as a predictor. They also added the rule "The ideal Dentist has a website" based on updated insight from current dental customers. A year after executing against these revised five Simple Rules, the company was realizing a 42% increase in sales in a tough market. Impressive!

A Global Manufacturer

A global manufacturer developed a set of Simple Rules to help them prioritize the work of designing, developing, and rolling out a complex Customer Relationship Management program. At a high level, the company's leadership team needed the Program Team to target its execution in an outcomes-based way; regularly delivering value and other actionable outcomes was key. Working together, the manufacturer and its Systems Integrator outlined the following Simple Rules:

- Our number one priority is outcomes; all other priorities related to costs, schedules, resources, quality, training, and value must support Priority One.

- Designing, developing, and rolling out a solution for the current scope is king; white space may be explored only after the current scope is deployed.

- We will deliver usable value to the business at least every six months and strive for incremental value at least quarterly.

- We will intentionally and rapidly prototype to learn and provide value more quickly; if we never fail, then we are not moving fast enough.

This Book

Once the proposal and draft Table of Content was developed, we used a brief set of Simple Rules to drive content development.

- Each chapter will comprise at least 8 but no more than 15 pages.

- Chapters will only drill down two levels/headings to minimize complexity.

- Words will be easily understood or *consumable* by a global and therefore diverse audience.

- The content will be formatted or delivered for rapid uptake and understanding.

- The content needs to align to the Project Management Institute's (2017) guidelines except in cases where Design Thinking drives a natural addition or slight adaptation.

- The team will work through the structure and chapter content iteratively, applying our Design Thinking model and chapter-specific Design Thinking techniques along the way as we work to create our "deliverable."

Consider the use cases noted in this section as starting points for thinking and ideating. Bring your team together sooner rather than later to begin drafting the team's very own Simple Rules. And remember, don't think *too much and too long* before beginning. Draft to think!

Effectively Adapting to Change through Guiding Principles

Guiding principles are succinct one-liners that serve as universal guardrails. These guardrails keep us focused—and in our lane—just as real guardrails do for cars on roads. Guiding Principles reflect what we value (i.e. our core values) along the lines of operational excellence or transparency in decisions or honesty in deal making.

Guiding Principles are the non-negotiable values and parameters that describe us and how we come to work each day.

Thus, Guiding Principles should not change much over time. For the purposes of this book, Guiding Principles are the "How" we execute or operate more so than the "Who" we are. A good Guiding Principle combines a core value with a verb that that reflects our world:

- We *execute* with transparency

- We *operate* with honesty

- We *work* with an eye towards achieving operational excellence.

As we covered earlier, let's create Simple Rules to describe our "Who" and "What." Then we can develop and apply Guiding Principles to bring together the "How" and the verbs which together describe how we aim to function and serve.

Responding to Changes

The Guiding Principles we provide throughout this book help us fast-track our thinking and make organizationally consistent decisions as we navigate the Program or Project roadmap. Use them as starting points. If we establish the right set of Guiding Principles for our Program or Project, we can quickly respond to changes in strategy, in the environment, in our staffing models, and more. Guiding Principles give us that head-start we need to avoid losing precious time; they help us quickly gain buy-in as we seek to make and implement the right decisions for us as a Program, Project, workstream, or team.

Probing for Understanding

The long-time MIT academic Kurt Lewin noted that the best way to understand something was to try to change it. Users will flock to help you understand why the current state is fine and why change is therefore unnecessary, for example. Conversely, other users will also flock to explain why a change fails to solve their problems. Either way, *these reactive communications help us grow in our understanding*. But this kind of ad hoc growth does not build broad understanding or drive empathy in a user-centric sustainable way.

Instead, we should **Probe for Understanding**. When we probe and ask deep questions to understand a situation, we are looking:

- Into the past, as a way to explain how we got here
- At the present, to assess why things are the way they are
- Towards the future, to think through what might happen when we introduce change

We probe by asking questions that cannot be answered without some thought. The goal is to bring more clarity to a situation, whether current or potential, to avoid mistakes that have been made before and to find a way through the ambiguity ahead of us.

Probing questions must go beyond questions that only clarify, though; probing questions are used to seek and understand the *edges* of a situation. For this reason, they are generally open-ended and often preceded with "Why...?"

Importantly, probing questions are not intended to eliminate all ambiguity! Complex and unique Programs and Projects will *always* reflect a degree of ambiguity. It is expected. Nor would we want to invest the time and energy trying to eliminate *all* ambiguity... such exercises are futile for complex endeavors.

Those who try to expose all complex Program/Project ambiguity either never complete anything or do so at such a high cost that the journey and its outcomes are not worth the investment.

Our goal is to simply cut through the first "layers" of ambiguity so we can be smarter as we finally set about iterating through something new.

Creating our Guiding Principles

Once we have an agreed-upon set of Simple Rules and an overall sense of understanding, we need to assign our Simple Rules the *verbs* that help us think and agree on "How" we will execute. This process will help us create our Guiding Principles, which in turn will allow us to move and address situations and questions more quickly and with consistency.

- If our Simple Rule is: "We will create something easily consumed by a global audience."

    o Then our Guiding Principle might be: "Avoid overly complex sentences and culture-specific colloquialisms"

- If our Simple Rule is: "We will help our readers maintain focus."

    o Then our Guiding Principle might be: "Spell out important acronyms again and again in each chapter as they are used."

- If our Simple Rule is: "The content will be formatted or delivered for rapid uptake and understanding."

    o Then our Guiding Principle might be: "Pictures and figures will be favored when many words would otherwise be necessary."

Simple Rules and Guiding Principles will naturally overlap a bit. We can combine them pretty easily, too, as you saw above. But overlapping and combining tells us we may have an opportunity to clarify the Rule or the Principle or both.

Like Simple Rules, we need to create our Guiding Principles as a team. The Executive Steering Committee, the PMO, the Architecture Review Board, the Change Control Board, the various Quality Management teams, the Test Team, and others should draw up their own respective Guiding Principles (supporting their respective set of Simple Rules).

Guiding Principles for Creating our Rules and Principles

To create a brief set of useful Simple Rules or Guiding Principles, consider the following Guiding Principles:

- Align Simple Rules to the "What" and Guiding Principles to the "How."

- Avoid the temptation to create Rules and Principles solo; worthwhile creation is a team endeavor executed best through **Hackathons** and **Brainstorming** activities.

- The Team that lives by the Rule should develop that Rule; avoid developing Rules for other teams!

- **Brainstorm** to create an initial pool of Simple Rules and Guiding Principles; then look for themes to help consolidate Rules and Principles into a number few enough to operate by.

- Every Simple Rule needs to be supported by one or more Guiding Principles; a one-to-many relationship is most common.

- More than five or six Simple Rules becomes cumbersome (and more easily forgotten and harder to live out long-term).

- There is no limit to the number of Guiding Principles, though the notion of core values dictates fewer rather than greater numbers.

- Simple Rules will change over time (less so for task-focused teams)

- Guiding Principles are less susceptible to change, again given their enduring core values nature.

Summary

This chapter introduced the role and importance of Simple Rules and Guiding Principles. The former describes who we are and what we do, and the latter describes how we do it. Simple Rules can change over time as our mission and vision change, but Guiding Principles tend to be more enduring in the same way that organizational core values are enduring. In the end, Simple Rules and Guiding Principles will help us preserve who we are, help us deliver what we are tasked to deliver, and help consistently perform the "how" of executing to deliver.

All of the Design Thinking techniques explored here and elsewhere are outlined in Appendix B, *Design Thinking Techniques*, starting on p. 196.

Case Study

One of the teams supporting the Harmony business transformation program needs help defining Who they are, What they do, When they do it, and How they should operate. You have suggested to the Team's supervisor a working session to identify Simple Rules and Guiding Principles that align with the overall Program and its Component Projects.

Chapter 4 Questions

1. Why shouldn't the Team's supervisor simply draft the initial set of Simple Rules solo?

2. How should you help differentiate between Rules and Principles?

3. What is the recommended process for reducing the number of Rules or Principles down to a manageable number?

4. Why would Guiding Principles be less susceptible to change over time than Simple Rules?

See Appendix A starting on p. 187 for Case Study answers.

PART II

Getting Ready

Chapter 5

Communications

- o *Design Thinking for Communications Management*
- o *Empathy through Listening*
- o *Applying Design Thinking to Artifacts*
- o *Questioning Deeply*
- o *Communicating Visually*
- o *Telling Stories*
- o *Prototyping Methods and Channels*
- o *Empathy through Realized Changes*
- o *Guiding Principles for General Communications, Meetings & Con-Calls, Team Communications, and Executive Communications*
- o *Chapter Summary and Case Study*

In this chapter, we look at how Design Thinking can improve both the standardized and ad hoc kinds of activities we must do in the name of Program and Project communications (Figure 5.1).

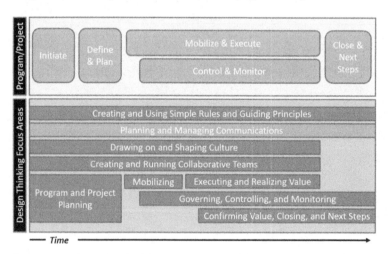

Figure 5.1 Apply Design Thinking to Communications throughout the lifecycle.

The Project Management Institute (2017) calls this *Communications Management*, and it is one of 10 key Knowledge Areas. As we see in Figure 5.1 above, communications are necessarily broad, spanning the Program or Project lifecycle end-to-end. This means we have the opportunity to influence and inform communications through Design Thinking across a Program's or Project's entirety!

Design Thinking for Communications Management

Always a top priority, Program and Project communications need to be executed superbly, and those communications must also be planned, managed, and monitored. The Project Management Institute (2017) shares that "Project Communications Management is the process of planning, collecting, storing, and updating project information...to ensure that the information needs of the project and its stakeholders are met through development of artifacts and implementation of activities designed to achieve effective information exchange."

A tremendous number of artifacts will be created to initially communicate, and other artifacts will be created over time to facilitate ongoing communications:

- **Planning:** Program and/or Project Charters, vision and mission artifacts, problem statements, project management plans and schedules, training schedules, and so on

- **Managing:** Communications management plan, stakeholder maps and registers, risks and issues plans and registers, dependency maps, program/project deliverables, training artifacts, and other items used in execution and management

- **Monitoring:** Dashboards and various levels of status reports spanning Sponsors and stakeholders to business leads, technology specialists, project team members, partner organizations, and others

All of these artifacts and methods for communicating are captured in the Communications Management Plan. Rather than explore these types of artifacts one-by-one and essentially repeat much of the guidance over and over again, we have organized this chapter around a number of Design Thinking tools or methods:

- Empathy through Listening

- Questioning Deeply

- Brainstorming the Critical or Enduring

- Communicating Visually

- Communicating through Stories

- Prototyping Methods and Channels

- Empathy through Realized Changes

Each of these Design Thinking methods are explored next, followed by a collection of Guiding Principles organized around General, In-Person, Team, and Executive or Stakeholder communications.

Empathy through Listening

Larry King once observed "Nothing I say this day will teach me anything. So, if I'm going to learn, I must do it by listening." The act of listening creates a meaningful shared communications foundation that can be built upon over time.

There is arguably no better way to learn and empathize than through listening to another's experiences and stories and unsolicited felt pain.

Listening takes a number of forms. Initially, we want and need to listen across a wide spectrum to those willing to talk. Eventually we will learn to filter the nuggets from the noise... but excluding anyone with a voice in the beginning does not make sense. The most vocal are often the most affected or interested, after all.

And we must listen across a breadth of audiences, too, from executives and other stakeholders to those on the front lines who have tried and failed... to those in business and IT roles... to leaders in other parts of the organization who have their own "edge" or outside perspectives... and to partners and others also on the edge or outside who may have special or unique insight.

Prior to and as we listen to others, we need to intentionally:

- **Know what we Need.** Think about the information you need and who might be in a position to share that information. More importantly, think deeply about whether you're seeking "ah ha" revelations, lessons learned, a history or debrief, feedback on recent events, thoughts on future ideas, or something else.

- **Choose and be Chosen.** Consider the balance between purposefully finding and sitting down with an audience vs also being open to having your audience find and sit *you* down. Nuggets come from both avenues.

- **Be Present.** There is nothing worse than a presumed listener failing to listen (as we all know from experience, it is all too easy to tell when our audience is distracted). Put away the smart phone, shut the lid to your laptop, find a good place without distractions, and be present. Listen and learn and *actually take notes* to ensure you do not forget what you are hearing/learning.

- **Be Self-Aware.** Listening also means responding real-time to *show* you're engaged, or thinking, or learning. Nodding your head subtly can be useful, as are simple words of affirmation, but do not over-use these techniques! We all know people who pretend to listen when in fact they are not, and we all know people who listen in such distracting ways that we cannot help but wonder if they are really listening.

Know yourself—your ticks and your habits—and regulate them to not only become a more effective listener but to avoid distracting the very people you most need to learn from and empathize with.

Applying Design Thinking to Artifacts

To apply Design Thinking in a smart way to the plans, documents, models, and other artifacts created through the life of a Program or Project, it is important to understand how an artifact will be used.

Consider employing an initial **Hackathon** to draw up an **Artifact Chart** detailing the artifact's primary and secondary audiences, goals, and outcomes desired for each artifact. Then identify the type of artifact (controlled, point-in-time, enduring, or living, all of which are explored next); work backwards to determine format, channel, structure, modularity, available templates, and reusable content; and finally apply Design Thinking practices potentially including another **Hackathon** to kick-start the artifact's development.

Controlled Artifacts

On the surface it would appear that any artifact by its very nature as a communications tool would benefit from **Rapid Prototyping** and iterating among other Design Thinking methods. But in the case of highly regulated or controlled artifacts such as security designs or HIPPA-influenced solution documents or ITAR-compliant architectures, teams are better off using **Standardized Templates**. Why? To ensure we do not either miss or alter something and get ourselves into trouble.

Point-in-Time Artifacts

On the other hand, artifacts such as a Program Charter, Milestone Chart, Benefits Register, and Stakeholder Register are typically built once and referred to often, though by a limited audience. Given this usage pattern and type of user community, we are probably better off putting together a small team and quickly building and iterating on a **Standardized** document **Template** in the early days until we become convinced we will not need to iterate again. With the exception of a bit of intentional iterating, then, such point-in-time artifacts line up closer with old-school plan and build models than Design Thinking "build to think" models.

Enduring Artifacts

Complex artifacts that are sure to change slightly over time benefit from a "building to think" perspective. Such artifacts are known as enduring artifacts. The master Project Plan, Solution Design documents, various Training artifacts, and other complex plans, documents, and artifacts benefit from early **Brainstorming** and **Ideating** and **Prototyping**. Why? Because audiences rather than individuals will use and live by these artifacts, and therefore those audiences need to weigh in *and* buy-in to how their respective artifacts are structured and built. Building enduring artifacts in this way will make inevitable maintenance that much easier (both politically and physically).

Enduring artifacts benefit from ongoing user-centric **Empathy**, Iterating (don't forget **The Rule of Threes**), and special attention to structure. Regarding structure, consider **Modularity** or creating content blocks in modules that can be combined and recombined for future related artifacts or documents.

Enduring artifacts must also reflect a level of user consensus around the volume of expected changes. Consensus minimizes the fall-out from making changes down the road.

It is much easier to change artifacts when the artifact's users were involved in the initial design and structure decisions in the first place.

With regard to enduring artifacts, consider the ubiquitous Project Plan....think about its structure and the way it is laid out in general, the way it is integrated within a larger Program or alongside other Component Projects, the way it is organized by workstream or phase or team, and the level of detail built into it. All of these structure details create a level of *consumability* by the users of the artifact; changes can become massive headaches to many people if the underlying structures have not been created to facilitate change. The Project Plan and other enduring artifacts such as training videos need to be planned and structured well and yet be flexible enough or modular enough to support necessary inevitable changes.

Living Artifacts

Some artifacts are destined to change quite frequently, and like enduring artifacts these living artifacts also benefit from user-centric **Empathy** and insight, building to think, **Rapid Prototyping** and iterating, and attention to structure and **Modularity**. Consider dashboards and status reports and detailed training materials—changes in both format and content will occur frequently in the beginning, and in the name of continuous improvement those changes may still be commonplace later in the Program or Project lifecycle.

Deep Questioning

As we strive for greater understanding on the journey towards empathy and better solutioning, we need to ask deep questions... the kind that really help us understand the mindset of a user or audience. Start with the **Five Why's**. The most basic question we can ask a user is "why," followed by "why" and "why" and "why" and "why." If we fail to **Probe for Understanding** as to why a person does something today, or fail to learn how that "something" came to be, we may never quite understand the nuances that capture a user's struggles, their current workarounds, and other behaviors.

We also need to drive our audience's or user community's participation. There are few better ways than asking good open-ended questions. Such questions drive thinking and reflection. Keep in mind that we need to:

- Give an interviewee or audience the freedom, space, and time to think; do not prematurely answer your own questions or lead your audience down a path.

Allow questions to sit and sink in and be answered in their own time. Be patient. Chances are you will be rewarded with fresh insights.

- Use provocative questions sparingly; avoid bombarding an audience with too many tough questions intended to illicit strong reactions.

- Balance the need to perform basic fact-finding with the need to be led down unexpected learning paths; the real rewards will come with the latter.

- Avoid jumping to conclusions; jumping interrupts the flow of information and frustrates the communicator as it implies you think you already have all the answers or are bored. Listen!

- Use your listening skills to identify the right clarifying questions. Clarification will improve both understanding and empathy.

- Show engagement throughout the communications process. Provide thoughtful and authentic feedback to answers to your questions to show you are listening. Echo especially important aspects of a response or experience or story as a way to reinforce the communicator's message or invite further detail.

Don't be a know-it-all! Rather, seek instead to be known as a listen-to-it-all.

Communicating Visually

We all know that complex ideas and processes are often best communicated visually. Visual communication refers to using pictures, figures, graphs, illustrations, diagrams, videos, and other media along the lines of "a picture is worth a thousand words." *Gantt Charts* are a long-time mainstay for illustrating Project schedules, for example.

Good visualizations reveal dependencies and simplify conditions and relationships with more economy and clarity than words.

Beyond pictures, figures, and graphs, use *animated content* and videos to communicate complex processes effectively and with repeatable consistency. It comes as no surprise that training videos trump text-heavy documents in terms of consumability and understanding. Such methods give end-users a consistent and repeatable "walking alongside me" approach for learning complex processes.

Finally, consider the use of **Structured Text** when words are still deemed the best method for communication. Structured text is great for step-by-step instructions. Structured text considers how we use formatting, physical placement, margins and other whitespace (literally the space around words), along with text highlighting and color to drive consumability and to elicit meaning.

- Whitespace. Place key words in a format that naturally draws the eye to them; writers need to employ their best System 2 (deep and slow) thinking to illicit a reader's System 1 (fast or automatic) response (Kahneman, 2011).

- Bullets. Create a set of bulleted items to help consolidate thinking or themes.

- Numbering. Use numbered lists to walk through a process step by step (1, 2, 3...).

- Consistency. Start your bullets in the same way with verbs (Perform, Execute, Review...) or gerunds (Performing, Executing, Reviewing...).

- Style. Use bold fonts or color sparingly, so you can truly draw an audience's attention when you really need it.

- Color. Apply color or highlighting to text sparingly to draw attention to that text.

With these tips in mind, many of the positive attributes of a good figure or picture can be built into a text-heavy artifact. We use this approach when we do not have a handy visual or screen shot at our disposal.

Telling Stories

Story telling is about uniting the right (creative) side of the brain with the left (logic) to produce emotionally sticky and memorable outcomes. When it really matters, and the time is available, stories help our messages not only "stick" but resonate in ways that other mediums cannot.

> *Stories change perceptions and biases. In this way, stories also change people and shape cultures.*

Good stories employ characters that matter, plots that are relevant, arcs that move with intentionality, and outcomes that surprise and delight. Stories follow a theme that can ultimately be summarized in a single word such as truth, or courage, or love. The theme is what continues to resonate in an audience's minds and hearts long after the words are read or spoken; it's usually the theme that drives the stickiness of the story.

Good stories do not "tell" but rather "show" through the story itself. You should rarely have to explain, for example, that such and such was important to you, or that you were thinking so and so, or that you felt a certain way. Instead, work on describing the experience well enough that the audience sees what you saw and feels what you felt.

In this way, when we need to grab attention and keep it for the long term, we must think about the power of stories. Use stories when we:

- Kick-off a new Program, Project, phase, or initiative

- Train our teams, our stakeholders, and above all our end-users

- Need to share a hard lesson with a team

- Wish to communicate an idea that needs to be retained long-term, just below the surface, influencing and informing decisions and actions in the most subtle of ways.

Stories have power. Just be sure to use them appropriately and sparingly enough to retain an audience's attention long enough to reap that power.

Stories are rarely a good fit for Sponsor and other executive stakeholder status updates, for example, especially in the midst of an escalation.

Prototyping Methods and Channels

When it comes to deciding how we will communicate with one another, there is no shortage of good ideas and bad ideas. Ideally, the team should brainstorm and discuss the available methods or channels, and then create a short list of those most likely to be easily used or readily consumed.

The key is for the team to find the way that the team actually *likes* to communicate. When teams are comprised of diverse members with diverse backgrounds, experiences, and so on, the ideal communication method or channel will be less apparent. This makes discussion of communications important, and it makes prototyping communications methods even more important.

Use **Rapid Prototyping** and **Hackathons** to work through a variety of communications tools, methods, and approaches. Create the team's initial list of options reflecting what the team agrees is feasible for them *today* and what is possible or should be further prototyped and tested in the near-term and mid-term.

In-person communications are ideal, of course, but often not possible given schedules, time-zones, and basic location logistics and travel expenses. Working with users and leaders, create a short-list of several alternatives when face-to-face communications is not feasible. Ask for lightweight **Mock-Ups**, **Demonstrations**, or **Pilots** to be executed if the frontrunner is unclear, and ensure actual users are engaged throughout the process including final evaluations. Options might include:

- Video-capable meeting software such as Teams, WebEx, Skype, Slack, Google Duo, Apple Facetime, and others

- Voice-only phone and phone app alternatives including WhatsApp, Viber, Talkatone, TalkU, WeTalk, etc

- Any number of Instant Messaging options

- Collaboration tools such as Microsoft Yammer

- Recorded videos shared via Web pages, Teams, or through apps

- Recorded Microsoft PowerPoint slides with voice-over

- Good old-fashioned Email and email distribution lists

- Updates provided through Web pages and forms

- Program/project-stylized Newsletters shared via email, Teams, Yammer, Web pages, and other means

Keep in mind we are not trying to create an exhaustive list above. Tools and techniques will come and go. Determine what your specific audience *needs* in terms of accessibility, persistence, consumability, and other attributes, and investigate the options available. And again, involve them in reviewing and evaluating the options.

Also consider how software solution-specific tools (such as GitHub, Azure DevOps, AWS Cloud9, Atom, or others used by software developers) can be extended to provide a communications platform inclusive of nondevelopers as well. Software partners such as SAP, Microsoft, and Oracle use specific platforms for developing their specific solutions. Such tools provide a persistent and traceable repository for communications and status, and they can oftentimes be used to create amazing charts and graphs and other graphics useful for communicating complexity.

Empathy through Realized Changes

At the end of the day, when we finally change systems, processes, and artifacts for the better, the work and outcomes are noticed. And if the work is done collaboratively and iteratively, with the right level and timing around training, it is appreciated. Sure, too much change can be counter-productive, so we need to balance keeping artifacts and processes static with making changes to those artifacts and processes. But there are few better ways to build goodwill with our users than to deliver changes well. When users empathize with the people in the teams working on their behalf, we see **Empathy Through Realized Changes**; the empathy comes as a result of seeing the work and the real progress (no matter how small that progress might be). Empathy through realized changes flips the user/team source/target relationship and thus the flow of empathy, generating hard-fought goodwill in its wake while creating a better work climate.

Guiding Principles for General Communications

To help ensure sound and effective communications, consider using or adapting the following guiding principles:

- If it's not written down, it didn't happen or won't happen.

- Know when to tell Stories and when to be Concise.

- Fight like you're right but listen like you're wrong.

- Draw on your user's communications format(s) for maximum consumability and to drive a *One Team* look and feel.

- Be consistent and use the same format, fonts, application of bold/highlights, color-coding, and so on.

- Be timely and accurate; ensure your audience can rely on your communications.

- For running status email updates, "reply all" to your previous email to ensure you maintain the history and preserve everyone on the distribution list.

- In presentations, use meaningful figures, pictures, and short bullets until more detail is necessary; the more detail, the more people are reading the slides and not listening to you.

- Spell out new acronyms until you are sure the acronyms are part of your audience's shared vocabulary.

- To help take the pressure off of being 100% correct in highly volatile or fluid situations, conclude key regular written communications such as email-based Status Updates with an invitation to "Reply-all with clarifications, questions, additional information, or to be removed from this communication."

Guiding Principles for Meetings and Con-Calls

Meetings, workshops, focus group sessions, and other face-to-face or remotely facilitated communications consume a tremendous amount of time and therefore need to be carefully scheduled and executed. Consider the following guiding principles:

- Lay out a meeting schedule and stick to it.

- When scheduling ad hoc meetings, provide enough advance notice to give key participants a shot at attending.

- Embrace the notion of giving people back time by allowing potential participants to opt out of meetings.

- Always provide meeting agendas well in advance of the meeting itself; if there is no need for an agenda, perhaps the meeting is unnecessary as well...

- Share those agendas and pre-read material in a format that is familiar, intuitive, accessible, and therefore easily consumable; there should be no excuses for lack of preparedness.

- Identify the scribe or notetaker as the first order of business when the meeting commences; human memory is no substitute for the indelible.

- If there is no reason to capture meeting notes, the meeting may have been a waste of time; consider asynchronous channels of communication in the future.

- For meetings that include remote attendees, drive inclusion by asking them to share their thoughts first (Nadella, 2017).

- Know when to tell stories and when to be concise; otherwise you will lose people's attention and risk not getting to the other important matters that mandated a meeting in the first place.

- Draw out the quietest attendees and ask them what they think; everyone needs to feel invited (Nadella, 2017).

- Before the meeting ends, identify if a follow-up meeting is needed and try to schedule it then and there.

- Identify and agree on the communication channel for follow-up (including meeting notes and next steps).

- Shortly after a meeting concludes, share follow-ups and next steps using an agreed-on communication channel.

The most effective post-meeting communicators never let the fear of a couple of typos or grammar issues keep them from publishing meeting notes immediately after a meeting concludes. The trade-off in terms of rapid post-meeting follow-ups and actions is worth the occasional typo.

Guiding Principles for Team Communications

Several common guiding principles have emerged over the years with regard to successful or effective team communications:

- In the same way that a chain's strength is defined by its individual links, individual credibility, accuracy, and respect for others sets the bar for *team* credibility, accuracy, and respect.

- Managers and team leaders need to be seen actively communicating and supporting their people. It's in the *visibility* that communications and cultural norms are established.

- Tailor communications to your teams' *content* needs; share the information that your audience needs rather than the information that you want to share.

- Know your audience's *quantity* needs and strike the right balance between too little and too much information shared via a single communication.

- Involve fellow team members in making and communicating decisions.

- Know when to exercise face-to-face communications and when other channels are acceptable.

- Strive for consistent communications, and in cases where strategy and follow-on messaging and direction changes, be sure to share the "why" and the "when."

- In the absence of the "why" and the "when," people will tend to fill the communications void with their own ideas and fears; minimize the voids.

- Repeat key messages; for urgent or critical communications, use more than one communications channel to ensure the message lands. And in this way, repeat those key messages.

- When "pinging" a team member over Instant Messaging or a similar technology, do not simply just say Hi or Hello; save time and frustration by also briefly sharing what you need in that same initial ping. Doing so is respectful, effective, and enables the respondent to think through your needs before responding.

Guiding Principles for Executive Communications

Given their limited time, bandwidth, and position in the organization, executives, Sponsors, and other stakeholders benefit from the following:

- Cover the urgent first; do not bury the bad news or build up to bad news through a story.

- Give yourself time to validate status and statements and their accuracy prior to communicating to executives and stakeholders.

- Sharing detailed Program or Project status is less important than making room for the executive decisions that need to be made.

- Communicate in as few words (or pages or slides) as necessary, until more words (or pages or slides) are absolutely necessary.

- Communicate in a way that demonstrates understanding of the executive's or stakeholder's expectations.

- Communicate in the executive's preferred format and with consistency using pictures, figures, charts, bullets, and intentional white space (**Structured Text**).

- Communicate in facts and with the right level of detail reflecting status, dates, responsible parties, milestones, risks, and issues.

- Spell out acronyms until you're sure they are part of an executive's vocabulary.

- Above all, listen. Document and act on feedback, and then follow up quickly to communicate progress and preserve credibility.

Summary

This chapter introduced us to ways to ways of thinking about and applying Design Thinking to Program and Project communications. We reviewed what it means to develop various communications artifacts and to select and use different communications methods or channels. We concluded with a set of Guiding Principles organized around general principles, in-person meetings, team communications, and executive or other stakeholder communications.

All of the Design Thinking techniques explored here and elsewhere are outlined in Appendix B, *Design Thinking Techniques*, starting on p. 196.

Case Study

The team is three months into the Program, and Harmony seems to be struggling with communications on a number of different fronts. You have been asked to share how Design Thinking might be applied to the Program's communications management processes and methods, especially those involving basic status updates, executive team updates, and regular stakeholder communications.

Chapter 5 Questions

1.   What are the seven Design Thinking areas outlined in this chapter that could be useful to improving communications?

2.   Beyond pictures and figures, what other kinds of visual communications aids might be useful?

3.   To what extent might stories prove useful in communicating basic status updates or executive or other stakeholder updates?

4.   How is "empathy through realized changes" a departure from how empathy is typically manifested in Design Thinking?

See Appendix A starting on p. 187 for Case Study answers.

Chapter 6

Drawing on and Shaping Culture

o   The Onion, the Snail, and the Cube
o   How Culture and Design Thinking are Interconnected
o   How Culture affects Practices and Concepts
o   Assessing and Shaping Culture
o   Understanding Cultural Intelligence
o   Guiding Principles for Drawing on and Shaping Culture
o   Chapter Summary and Case Study

Before we travel too far down the path of implementing a Program or Project, we need to consider culture. Culture affects and informs the bulk of the Program and Project lifecycle (Figure 6.1), from individual and team attitudes to organizations, geographies, and other dimensions. Culture needs to be *drawn upon* to effect near term change, and it needs to be intentionally and actively *shaped* to help our Programs and Projects achieve their intended long-term transformation goals.

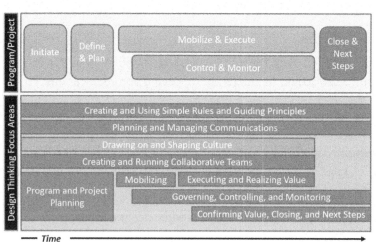

Figure 6.1 Drawing on and Shaping Culture starts immediately.

The Onion, the Snail, and the Cube

Culture is shaped every day by the actions and words and attitudes shared by every individual in an organization (Nadella, 2017). Culture comprises both our unique *and* our shared experiences, attitudes, behaviors, biases, communication styles, work styles, perspectives, preferences, and other attributes (Figure 6.2).

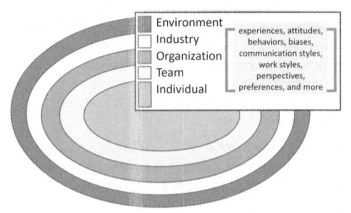

Figure 6.2 Culture is like an onion in that they're both Layered.

Together, like the layers of an onion, these attributes inform and shape each person, each team, and every organization in every industry across a broader macro-economic and political environment.

This shaping takes time; culture changes slowly, like a snail making its way on a journey. Like the snail, culture is organic and alive, slow to move and change, and it is amorphous and messy (Figure 6.3). Culture reflects the countless attributes introduced, changed, and removed over time by people as they join and leave a team and broader organization.

Figure 6.3 The analogy of the Culture Snail.

Beyond its layers and slow-moving nature, culture is also multi-dimensional and complex. Hundreds of models have been pulled together over the years to explain and organize culture and its dimensions. Many of these models are based on what it means for organizations to change, including Burke-Litwin's detailed 10-component change model and Kotter's well known 8-step model for change.

Other models organize culture around important organizational dynamics or components, from Hofstede's 6-dimension Multi-Focus culture model to Miller's 16 Dynamics of Culture, Ross's Communication-Unity-Leadership model, Denison's 4-quadrant organizational culture model, and Schein's broadly accepted Organizational Culture model and supporting work spanning six decades.

For our purposes here as we consider what it means to apply Design Thinking to Program and Project Management, let us condense culture into a three dimensional cube reflecting eight overall perspectives or dynamics (see Figure 6.4).

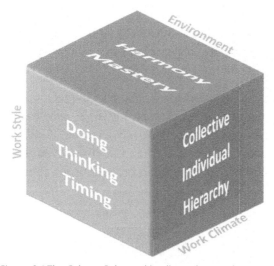

Figure 6.4 The Culture Cube and its dimensions and perspectives.

Our three culture dimensions are Environment, Work Climate, and Work Style. The first two align clearly to layers in the Culture Onion (where work climate is synonymous with "Team").

- **Environment.** How people think about their overall workplace.
  - Harmony, or the ability to work and relate with one another effectively in the workplace.
  - Mastery, or the desire to continually improve at something that matters and is therefore meaningful (Pink, 2009).
- **Work Climate.** How people work with and relate to one another.
  - Collective, or the extent to which a team works effectively together, values people and/or the work being done, and shares similar ideas of goals and success.
  - Individual, or what each team member personally brings to a team in terms of background, experience, biases, values (and respect, initiative, leadership "follow-ship" styles, empathy, conflict management skills, and more).
  - Hierarchy, or the "vertical differences between team members" (Greer, 2018) spanning teams and the overall organization.
- **Work Style.** How and when people get things done.
  - Doing, or how and why work is executed and the extent to which the work is strictly structured and governed (or not).
  - Thinking, or the planning performed before work is executed.
  - Timing, or when work is executed.

Culture moves slowly and in subtle ways, reflecting changes with every new-hire brought to a team and every gap left when someone leaves.

These individual plusses and minuses therefore slowly affect and change an organization's culture in terms of the overall environment, the more tactical work climates of each team, and the observed work styles both within and *between* each team.

Individual Culture and Team/Work-Climate Considerations

Every individual of every team affects how that team performs. It is the job of culture-aware leadership to understand individual attributes and team dynamics such that culture can be drawn upon, leveraged, and shaped or nurtured. These individual attributes include:

- **Personal background.** Probably the most complex of all potential individual differences, unacknowledged or disrespected differences in backgrounds, languages, communication styles, religions, customs, clothing, food preferences, family perspectives, and similar can quickly wreak havoc on a team.

- **Personal work experience.** Individual work experience levels, including work experiences gained outside of the specific role a person may hold today, inform how that person thinks and the assumptions they make.

- **Personal biases.** The known, unknown, and unrealized biases and specific behaviors that people bring to the workplace either intentionally or by default.

- **Personal emotional intelligence.** Emotional self-awareness and the ability to manage and control those emotions based on the specific and unique needs of an environment; includes social skills, humility, empathy, respect for others, motivation, and drive (Goleman, 1998). Motivation and drive are also synonymous with *hunger* and an aggressive can-do attitude.

- **Personal cultural intelligence.** The capacity of a person to adapt to new cultural settings and to interact effectively with people from different cultures or diverse backgrounds or lifestyles; akin to self-awareness and self-regulation combined with the ability to fit in and to understand and respect the differences in others (detailed later in this chapter).

Leaders need to pay attention to their teams in terms of what is functioning *well* and what seems to be dysfunctional, and then actively ideate and manage the changes necessary to address the dysfunctional while reinforcing the functional. As Edgar Schein of MIT's Sloan Management of School said, "The only thing of real importance that leaders do is create and manage culture. If you do not manage culture, it manages you…" (2010).

Country and Geographic Considerations

Cultural realities of the country or geographic location in which we find ourselves working must be understood, respected, and accommodated. The breadth of this understanding and respect includes:

- **Local work rules.** Daily work schedule, mandatory or voluntary overtime, and shift differential compensation need to be considered.

- **Religious considerations.** Be aware of the religious customs, traditions, and special observances that are celebrated by various team members and stakeholders. For instance, take into consideration such matters when scheduling a Project cutover or Program phase kick-off that occurs at a time when the necessary team members or stakeholders might simply not be available.

- **Economic differences.** Though it is nearly impossible to enforce, create a culture where salary and rewards discussions take a back seat to challenging work and great teams. Given the diversity in large transformational Programs and their teams staffed by individuals hailing from every corner of the globe, expect significant economic differences.

- **Political differences.** Like religious and economic differences, geographically disbursed Program and Project teams will also represent a variety of political perspectives. Respect differences and actively seek to avoid situations where differences might divide teams.

- **Holidays and other local realities.** Consider how Regional, National, State/Province, and Local holidays will affect your team, along with norms in working days, geographic or country-specific clothing norms, differences in tax realities, import/export regulations, and other such matters.

How Culture and Design Thinking are Interconnected

When it comes to getting things done, culture trumps any desire we have to institute a "way" to think, including Design Thinking. Culture is like the force of gravity in that it is both weak and yet incredibly strong.

Culture reflects how we are pre-wired to think based on where we grew up, the places we have lived and worked, and the diversity we have observed and absorbed from the cultures and people around us.

In this truth lies several challenges that will affect not only our teams' default work styles, but how each person and each team approaches and applies Design Thinking to Program and Project Management.

- **Know our Defaults.** Each individual and every team represents a unique set of *default* perspectives, attitudes, biases, ways of working, and so on. We need to recognize the default behaviors and biases in ourselves and in our people.

- **Hierarchy.** How outspoken, comfortable, and aligned are our people when it comes to brainstorming aloud, feeling empowered to act without asking permission, escalating needs, making decisions, seeking guidance, or simply doing the hard work of completing something? Are they constrained by hierarchy or free from it? Or are they stuck somewhere in between?

- **Mode of activity.** To what extent does our team reflect a mix of classic Western *doing* and Eastern *thinking* and other manners of engaging? How does that unique mix affect our ability to "build to think" through **Brainstorming**, **Hacking**, **Prototyping** and experimenting, **Iterating**, and **Testing to Learn**?

- **Perception of time.** Which of our team members value schedules, agendas, and punctuality (a monochronic perspective)? Which view time as more fluid and deadlines as suggestions (a polychronic perspective)? And where do we have the need for time management training? Do other issues affect the team's perception of time, such as a lack of clarity around roles or the nature of the work itself?

We need to work with our team members and particularly our leaders to intentionally improve Work Style cultural awareness as we go about our style of Doing, Thinking, and Timing. We need to not only recognize natural tendencies but help our teams break through their in-built default patterns. Consider how optimism bias, and conscious and unconscious biases, for example, affect how a team views the people around them and the work in front of them.

> *To target healthy changes, Leaders need to help their people and their teams recognize their default patterns and in-built biases.*

We need to become more adept at moving between monochronic and polychronic thinking, too. To a Program's or Project's advantage, we need to draw on our team members and others who think differently than our own default; if we are faced with a difficult non-negotiable work product deadline to meet, we are better off assigning that work product to one of our monochronic-centered team members. If our entire Project or Program comprises a series of hard deadlines (think "regulatory matters" or "security" or similar non-negotiable deadlines), we had better drive monochronic thinking throughout the team, too.

Finally, we need to find a balance between thinking, planning, and doing. There is a time and a place for deep System 1 thinking and "planning," and there is a time and a place for faster System 2 thinking and "doing" (Kahneman, 2011). We need to help our teams understand when they need to move slow *so they can move faster later*, and when (and why) they need to move fast or make decisions now, out of the gate, despite natural tendencies in stressful or ambiguous times to stop and analyze. It is in these stressful times that we must lean on our **Patterns, Simple Rules,** and **Guiding Principles** to help us wade through the unknowns.

How Culture affects Practices and Concepts

Of course, culture affects more than our norms around Doing, Thinking, and Timing. Culture also affects how we perceive and value words, practices, and concepts. The notion behind the word *prototype* specifically means *throw-away* in some cultures, for example. In yet other cultures, a prototype reflects a fixed set of requirements-based functionality to be built upon and eventually used as-is productively.

Similarly, innovation and innovative practices mean different things to different people and different cultures. Innovation might only mean "trying something new" with little value, or untested value, or at high-risk with low reward. Others may view innovations proudly regardless of immediate value.

Assignment tasking is viewed differently by different cultures, too. In hierarchical cultures, a critically important task might be assigned to a Team Leader or a particular team by virtue of position regardless of whether that particular person or team can do what needs to be done. In other parts of the world, the team or person with the most expertise is assigned regardless of hierarchy or position.

How people work, including the notion of cubicles, war rooms, private offices, and other workspaces also differs culturally. Consider the prevalence of Open Spaces in some countries versus the use of dedicated Project Spaces and offices in other countries. As we bring together our teams, we need to consider which of these will be most effective (and which of these we simply need to work around). Keep in mind that as the work changes and roles potentially change, what might have once been effective can evolve into a blocker to progress.

Finally, consider basic communications norms in the context of culture. In some cultures, it is commonplace and expected to jump in and interrupt others in meetings. People jockey and push to be heard and recognized. In other cultures, such actions are disrespectful and counterproductive. In yet other cultures, people stay quiet until called upon; we will have to draw out those team member's perspectives and ideas and ask for inputs. The point here? Be aware of who needs to be *pulled in* and who needs to be *moderated*.

Know your team and establish communications and other ground rules that create a culture of inclusion.

Drive curiosity, reward listening, and above all enforce respect for others. In doing so, you will create a safe place for questioning, experimentation, **Ideation**, and trying new Design Thinking techniques, and you will get the best out of your diverse teams and organizations.

Assessing and Shaping Culture

Our goal is not to try to change everyone on Day One of a Program or Project. After all, we know through common sense and experience that we cannot change culture by "changing culture."

Culture is changed or shaped a person at a time and a behavior at a time... and it takes time.

Instead, we should seek to first take the following broad-based steps:

- **Draw on the current culture.** The idea here is to meet our people and our teams where they are, just as we do when it comes to developing our people's capabilities or our organization's maturity. In this way, we can immediately use and build upon the most valuable *existing* aspects of our team's or organization's culture as we learn to work through existing patterns and biases and start building momentum and progress.

- **Intentionally evolve and shape culture.** Next, in parallel to drawing on the current culture to make initial progress, we need to shape and redefine over time what it means to be an effective team or a supportive organization. We need to promote specific attitudes, behaviors, and healthy biases, and squash others. And in doing so, we must consider how the current culture will react and evolve across the three dimensions of environment, work climate, and work style.

Our goal here is to gently push the culture to a place where differences are intentionally leveraged for *good* and take a back seat to achieving a Program's or Project's goals and objectives. We want to take steps to bring teams together, to reward work well-done, and to embrace the perspective that the right person for a particular assignment has nothing to do with differences but rather with capabilities, maturity, and attitude.

We must be careful not to inadvertently segregate or separate particular teams or departments from one another. The goal and the right thing to do is to drive *inclusion.* There are no outsiders on a Team, regardless of geographical boundaries or experiences.

And in cases where someone has infringed upon another's rights or created a less than safe work environment, we must take swift steps to address the problem and set a positive example—not just leaders, but everyone.

Helping one another bring the best that we can bring to work every day is not just a job for leadership; it is everyone's job and everyone's responsibility to look out for one another.

How and where do we start? The easiest way to assess our team's or organization's culture is to simply look around. What do people do? What seems to be the team's default and likely unwritten **Simple Rules** and **Guiding Principles**? How do people act? Which behaviors are tolerated, and which are not? What does the team prioritize and value? What is their track record for getting hard things done? Look and listen!

And pay attention to what other people say about the team—your team—and your organization here and now. These nuggets of solicited and unsolicited feedback and insight reveal an important point-in-time perspective. Such perspectives give us a baseline against which we can later measure our culture's evolution.

To assess today's culture and intentionally shape culture over time, consider this four-step process or exercise:

1. **Understand and baseline the present culture**

   - Assess individual and team behaviors and values as described above (and consider using a formal Culture survey or instrument).

   - Map these current behaviors and values to create a Current State model; this is our baseline.

2. **Model the future culture**

   - Describe a high-level future state based on the Program's or Project's business goals or organizational transformation's expected outcomes. What is our future vision? Who do we want to be, what should we value, and what does that look like from a behavioral perspective?

- Determine which behaviors and values support our future vision (that is, behaviors and values that need to be reinforced) and which need to change to achieve the vision (behaviors and values that need to be diminished, replaced, or outright eliminated).

3. **Develop a culture transformation roadmap and plan**

- Map all of these specific behaviors and values to create a Future State Behavior Model.

- Consider the organization's Simple Rules and Guiding Principles in the context of the Future State Behavior Model; what else needs to be changed so that the Who, What, When (our Simple Rules) and How (our Guiding Principles) align with our desired future culture?

- Agree on and document the key behaviors and values that must change.

- Create the Culture Transformation Roadmap and Plan, where for each behavior or value that needs to change there is a corresponding action (to increase B1, we will do or encourage X, Y, and Z; to increase V1, we will do ABC).

4. **Execute, evaluate, and iterate**

- Execute the actions in the Plan intended to change behaviors or values.

- Model the new values and behaviors top down.

- Make aware and train the team in the new behaviors and values, including answering the "why" behind each change.

- Reinforce good behaviors and expressions of new values.

- Evaluate progress and make course corrections iteratively as needed (quit doing X, increase Y, tweak Z...)

Understanding Cultural Intelligence

Much work has been done recently around the notion of *cultural intelligence* or the capacity of a person to adapt to new cultural settings and to interact effectively with people from different cultures or diverse backgrounds or lifestyles.

Cultural intelligence is akin to self-awareness combined with understanding and respecting the differences in others.

When leaders are more culturally aware or intelligent, they exhibit deeper empathy; practice better listening, decision making, and negotiation skills; build more trusting and trustworthy teams; and improve their leadership effectiveness. Stronger cultural intelligence in turn creates a safer place for communication, ideation, prototyping, testing, challenging assumptions, iterating, and practicing other **Design Thinking** techniques or processes across the team.

Strong cultural intelligence creates a safer and healthier pro-innovation work climate.

Cultural intelligence is measured by observing or asking questions related to a host of areas (many of which align to our Culture Cube's perspectives or dynamics). Key cultural intelligence dimensions relate to how we go about planning, decision making, communications, and collaborating; how we view time; how we value caring for self vs others; how we think about and work within a hierarchy; our thoughts around introducing and adopting changes; and how the needs of work rank against family, church and community, society, and other priorities.

By assessing ourselves and our teams in these areas, we can effectively "score" a person's or a team's cultural intelligence.

Knowing our cultural strengths is good, but understanding our gaps lets us intentionally improve team working dynamics and influence individual and team development plans.

Improvements in cultural intelligence leads to fewer misunderstandings, greater effectiveness, and improved health.

We have found that teams and team members who exhibit higher cultural intelligence ultimately trust one another more, leading to obvious benefits across their local teams and the broader Program or Project.

Look to one of the available online Culture Intelligence (CQ) surveys at https://www.aacu.org/ for examples of short but effective cultural intelligence questionnaires. CQ surveys allow you to self-assess (or assess a team's) cultural adaptability and effectiveness.

Leaders in particular need to take several steps to model healthy cultural intelligence. Doing so helps these leaders learn and grow, but more importantly helps their teams perform at higher levels while improving the overall workplace and its work products.

- Engage with your other time-zone mentors and colleagues more frequently and more intentionally to come away with fresh insights and different perspectives.

- Staff teams with an eye towards diversity, introducing new team members from other cultures and backgrounds who bring new perspectives and help the team experiment/ideate in new ways.

- Balance staffing young (with new insights and ways of thinking) with more senior or experienced team members (who can also bring an understanding around the history explaining our current state of affairs).

- Be aware of differences in the ways that team members perceive *context*; low context cultures tend to create more connections to others but with less depth or duration; similarly, low context cultures tend to rely less on non-verbal communications and more on discrete spoken or written messages with high clarity.

- Know when to toss aside all of this guidance and people's differences and simply treat one another as fellow humans and teammates. Take special care to avoid inadvertently stereotyping team members.

- Finally, when inevitable missteps are made, own those mistakes and model the kind of humility and genuine remorse consistent with transparent leadership and good citizenship.

*Transparent and culturally-aware Leadership
demands humility.*

With a sense of Cultural Intelligence in mind, let us synthesize this Chapter's learnings into a set of Guiding Principles. Remember that our goal is to immediately draw on or leverage our present culture while working in parallel to intentionally influence behaviors and values which in turn will shape our culture over time.

Guiding Principles for Drawing on and Shaping Culture

In the beginning, it is always more effective to draw on or leverage the current culture than to try to change it. Shaping culture takes months and years and good reasons to change; a transformational business program can surely be a driver, but as we all know culture change does not magically happen the day of Kick-Off.

- Cultural diversity brings strength, experience, unexpected capabilities, and multiplicity in thought; for these reasons, diversity should be treated as one of an organization's most valuable players (MVPs).

- Before you think about changing or shaping culture, take the steps necessary to understand how the *current* culture aids or hinders your goals (Schein, 2010).

- Draw on the strengths of the current culture rather than trying to overcome real or perceived constraints or diving too quickly into behavior and value changes.

- Culture change starts where people are today; you cannot accelerate culture change by jumping into the middle of the change process.

- Never be tempted to delegate or "outsource" change leadership (Gibbings, 2018); change needs to be owned by the Program's or Project's leaders and Sponsor.

- If you fail to understand or account for the layers of your culture and how these layers inform the broader culture inward and outward, you will be hard-pressed to make lasting change (refer to the Culture Onion, p. 91).

- Driving meaningful culture changes across teams means focusing awareness on Work Styles (Doing, Thinking, and Timing), Work Climate (Collective, Individual, and Hierarchy), and on the broader Environment (Harmony and Mastery).

- You cannot change culture by "changing culture;" you change behaviors and values a person at a time, over time.

- While the idea of "changing culture by changing culture" is flawed, there are indeed aspects of culture change that can be *accelerated* if there is a sufficient widely-held reason to change.

- Team and Organization culture changes with changes in staffing, a person at a time and a day at a time; use this dynamic well.

- People exhibit and prioritize a certain set of behaviors until they're incentivized to exhibit a different set of behaviors.

- People need time to unlearn how they behave or what they currently do or value before they can learn new behaviors and values (Heathfield, 2012).

- However, success can also "cause people to unlearn the habits that made them successful in the first place" (Nadella, 2017), replacing them with bad habits through lack of awareness or flagging empathy.

- Reinforce and model the *good* and gently correct everything else.

- If you do not actively and intentionally manage culture and its evolution, it will manage you (Schein, 2010).

Summary

This chapter presented culture considerations and realities, including the layers of culture (the Onion), a multi-dimensional way to organize and think about culture (the Cube) comprised of Environment, Work Climate, and Work Style dimensions, and a simple view into the nature of culture (the Culture Snail).

Next, we considered how culture and Design Thinking are interconnected, how culture affects Practices and Concepts, and how we can go about assessing current culture as a predecessor to influencing and shaping culture change. As usual, we concluded the Chapter with a set of Guiding Principles, in this case focused around drawing on and shaping culture.

All of the Design Thinking techniques explored here and elsewhere are outlined in Appendix B, *Design Thinking Techniques*, starting on p. 196.

Case Study

As a global organization, FAST and its teams are naturally culturally diverse. However, senior management and the Harmony PMO keep running into examples of poor collaboration, ineffective teaming, missed deadlines, and out of sync priorities. The Harmony Program Sponsor has asked you to look into this situation, as some of this behavior seems to be tied to a lack of cultural awareness or intelligence emanating from more than a few team members.

Chapter 6 Questions

1. How might we view our Program team's culture in terms of layers? What about dimensions?

2. What are the three dimensions of the Culture Cube and its eight perspectives or dynamics, and which of the eight perspectives or dynamics might help us explore cultural aspects of "missed deadlines?"

3. You have decided that a basic cultural assessment followed by intentional shaping is in order. What are four steps that you would take to initially assess and longer-term shape the Program team's culture?

4. In what kinds of ways might you measure or baseline the Program team from a Cultural Intelligence perspective?

See Appendix A starting on p. 187 for Case Study answers.

Chapter 7

Creating and Running Collaborative Teams

o   *The Effective and Collaborative Team*
o   *Accelerating Innovation: Diversity Teaming*
o   *Engaging Different Perspectives*
o   *Recognizing and Working through Biases*
o   *The Diversity Paradox*
o   *Role Clarity: Organizing around Outcomes*
o   *Team Velocity: Organizing for Speed*
o   *Additional Benefits of Diversity Teaming*
o   *Guiding Principles for Effective Teams and Workplaces*
o   *Chapter Summary and Case Study*

In this chapter, we investigate the case for creating diverse cross-boundary teams to drive effective innovation, ideation, and ultimately collaboration and outcomes. Creating and running these teams spans much of the Program and Project lifecycle (see Figure 7.1).

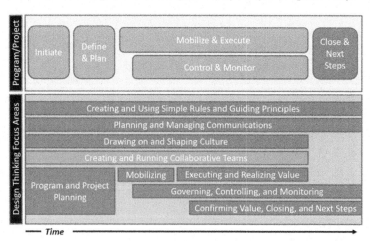

Figure 7.1 Use Design Thinking to create and run diverse and collaborative teams.

We also explore the notion of perspectives and the urgency to understand and work through biases. Then we walk through the Diversity Paradox and draw a welcome, if not surprising, conclusion. Next, we consider how to increase role clarity and team velocity, along with exploring views around the advantages and realities of diversity teaming. Chapter 7 concludes with a set of Guiding Principles aimed at creating more effective teams and therefore more collaborative work climates and workplaces.

The Effective and Collaborative Team

As we have said before, very few things worthwhile or enduring can be successfully completed solo; complex business transformations and other complex endeavors demand gifted teams to enable Programs and Projects to deliver their promised benefits and other outcomes.

But what makes an effective team? Said another way, how can we create a collaborative and healthy Work Climate (as discussed in Chapter 6) wherein people bring out the best in one another while getting the job done? As we will cover in the next several pages, effective teams require talented individuals who are not only capable of doing (while forever learning and refining their understanding of!) the work, but operate with the following characteristics and attitudes:

- Self-awareness and self-management (think "bias awareness")
- Courageous perspectives shared through respectful person-to-person communications
- A growth mindset that acknowledges learning requires trying and doing and yes, occasionally failing, on the way to achievement
- Strong initiative and enduring motivation
- Situationally-aware leadership and equally adept follower-ship
- Superb communications and conflict management skills
- The ability to work with anyone while helping one another grow

Teams that look back at their performance and apply feedback to improve their processes are effective teams. This "reflective" mode of team evolution models Design Thinking's principles regarding feedback loops, thoughtful iteration, and continuous improvement.

And finally, as we explored in Chapter 6 and the dimensions of the Culture Cube, effective teams require a supportive culture that promotes a healthy environment, work climate, and work styles. Let us now turn our attention to several of these attributes that accelerate or otherwise affect innovation and outcomes.

Accelerating Innovation: Diversity Teaming

Experience and two decades of research reveal this truth: diverse teams accelerate innovation (Forbes, 2011). This truth does not mean it is easy and it does not mean we will not face other challenges related to communications and culture covered. But it does mean that if we are looking for ways to think differently and solve really hard problems, we are better off pulling together a diverse or *cross-boundary* team.

Diverse or cross-boundary teams are those with team members, both men and women, who hail from different backgrounds, geographies, cultures, ethnicities, organizations, and disciplines... merging and working together to bring their unique experiences and perspectives to bear.

The greatest benefits of cross-boundary teaming are found in the options and the results that these teams deliver. Apply cross-boundary teaming across the *Design Thinking Model for Program and Project Management*, from broad understanding and user empathy exercises to problem definition, brainstorming, prototyping, testing, and deployment.

Engaging Different Perspectives

Bringing "different" perspectives to a problem is more difficult than it sounds. Our own biases and blindness get in the way.

*We become accustomed to tackling tough problems
by pulling together teams of our best and brightest.
Look around at the team. Do you see more
similarities than differences? Where's the diversity?*

If there is a lack of team diversity, from where will the differing perspectives and experiences come? And without those differing perspectives, from where will new thinking and new ideas come?

Think about the perspectives of a cylinder (Figure 7.2). One person may see it from above and will be convinced they see a circle. Another person might have a side perspective and be convinced they are viewing a rectangle. Another person might be a bit offset from the rest, though, and her perspective might rightly yield a view of a cylinder. We need a diverse team with multiple perspectives to simply *look* at a problem or situation in different ways (much less to bring a variety of potential solutions to the problem or situation). It is through our diversity that we can see what alone we cannot.

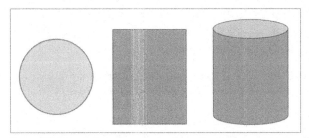

Figure 7.2 Note the varying perspectives of a Cylinder.

The circle, rectangle, and cylinder should remind us that hard problems are rarely solved singularly. It is better to have 10 views and 5 potential solutions than a single view and lone shot at solving a problem.

Recognizing and Working through Biases

Everyone is biased; we all have our preferences and default ways of thinking and responding. Biases come from what we have experienced and seen in the past, and they are manifested in the present as we apply those past experiences to how we work, communicate, collaborate, and make decisions. The key to working through biases is to know them, recognize them, and therefore be able to identify them in yourself. After all, *unintentional* biases hurt people and relationships (and teams and reputations) just as intentional biases do.

There are many forms of bias, but when it comes to working and behaving well within diverse teams, there are several forms of these *poor mental shortcuts* that can go overlooked:

- **Confirmation bias**, which occurs because people tend to believe (and want to believe) something that seems to confirm what we think we already know.

- **Action bias**, or the notion that it is better to do something than nothing...even in the absence of any understanding or information supporting that "something." The outcome is wasted time and effort. This bias may be seen in those eager to "build to think" and those uninterested in planning.

- **Bandwagon bias**, or the notion that an idea already floating around and adopted by others should be followed (rather than debated or simply set aside as we seek additional ideas).

- **Information bias**, which says that we still need more information to make the best decision (keeping us frozen or on the same course in the meantime).

- **Framing bias**, which occurs when a poor idea is adopted simply because it was presented really well.

- **Pro-innovation bias**, where new ideas are pushed simply because they are *new* and therefore presumed innovative.

- **In-group bias**, or the practice of dismissing out of hand the ideas that come from groups of people who differ from you in terms of culture or background or experience, skin color, height, weight, education, and infinitely other attributes....

Biases are not reserved for individuals only; they exist at a team level as well. For example, in-group bias will drive *teams* to favor their own ideas or thinking over other teams' ideas or thinking. Framing bias will drive a team or an individual to perceive a well-presented idea as perhaps the best idea. Teams, especially those expected to be innovative, will err on the side of action bias rather than risking the perception that they're "thinking (too much) to build." These biases have zero merit, yet they all too often influence our actions and those of our teams and organizations.

So be on the alert for biases! Biases shut down innovation, particularly ideation, prototyping, working through assumptions, and performing internal data gathering or feedback sessions. When you hear phrases such as "that will never get approved by the board" or "we tried that and it failed" or "nobody would want that," gently call out these statements as perceptions worthy of consideration but *reflective of the past*. Remind the team that we must learn from our mistakes but remain focused on the future.

> *Find ways of connecting empathy for what we have*
> *seen and heard with the desire to hear all*
> *perspectives—old and new alike.*

We need to keep communications open and flowing. After all, today's problems are never identical to yesterday's problems, nor can they always be solved by yesterday's solutions. And as we will see next, we have a much better chance at solving today's problems if we can draw on a broader and more diverse cross-section of potential ideas.

The Diversity Paradox

We already naturally know this, but to be clear, diverse teams are not an all-encompassing cure for driving innovation. Why? Because people are people... error-prone emotional humans subject to biases and default patterns that get in the way of bringing their best to work every day.

Beyond the typical (and expected) communication and culture challenges lies another important matter: the volume and quality of innovative outcomes. Specifically, there is a well-known trade-off between highly diverse teams and the number and value of their innovative outcomes (Flemming, 2007). The greater the team diversity:

- The greater the number of new ideas
- The greater the number of breakthrough innovations
- The greater the number of failures

- And statistically speaking, the *lower* the average value of the innovations realized

Read that list above again, though. We want new ideas; we need new ideas… some will be great and others not so great… and with those ideas we will naturally realize a mix of successes and learnings and failures.

The fact that the distribution of innovation successes for diverse teams yields more innovations at a bit lower average value is actually a welcome outcome compared to low-diversity teams yielding fewer ideas and even fewer innovations at a slightly higher average value per innovation.

Analogous to free market economics, Diversity Paradox outcomes *grow* the size of our pie (that is, our base of ideas). So, while the Diversity Paradox on the surface may seem to imply something adverse, the Paradox innately reflects a healthy overall consequence: a greater pool of ideas and subsequently a greater yield of innovative outcomes!

Role Clarity: Organizing around Outcomes

When it comes to role clarity, organize people by teams and around specific goals, outcomes, or responsibilities. In addition, consider how Programs and Projects are *matrixed* as a result of their virtual leadership teams, architecture boards, and so forth. Key virtual leadership teams include:

- Executive-Level Steering Committee

- Working-Level or Operational Steering Committee

- Architecture Review Board (to govern strategic technology decisions and direction)

- Change Control Board (to govern Program and Project scope changes)

- Benefits Realization or Quality Board (to track Program/Project benefits realization and the quality and timing of those benefits)

- Fit/Gap Review Board (to evaluate strategies, user implications, financial implications, and other matters related to filling in the gaps)

Membership in these Committees and Boards spans various teams, creating dotted-line or matrixed relationships for specific roles to one or more Committees or Boards. However, each role is formally tied to precisely one and only one team or home. In this way, we preserve clarity and a simple 1:1 hard-line relationship between all roles and every team. For example, roles might hard-line to one of the following:

- The Program Management Office (one per Program)

- The Project Management Office (one per Component Project)

- Architecture and Technology Team (may be shared)

- Change Management Team (to manage end-user change)

- Quality Assurance Team (deliverables, code, test cases, etc)

- Development or "Build" Team (create and initially test solutions)

- Functional Test Team

- Performance Test Team

- Functional Security Team

- Technical Security Team

- Audit Team

- Training Team

- Operations/Support and various Help Desk Teams

Team Velocity: Organizing for Speed

Beyond roles and team clarity, we need to operate our teams in a way that equips them to move quickly to reduce Time-to-Value while promoting healthy collaboration and teaming. Practices that align well with Design Thinking include the following:

- **Exercise and model trust.** Teams survive longer, move faster, and experiment and take smarter risks (which may or may not pan out, consistent with failing and learning fast) when individuals transparently believe in and trust one another.

- **Enforce accountability.** To preserve trust, we need to ensure that when our teams say they are going to do something that they are held to that promise. Consequences are a natural part of life; do not shy away from them but rather use consequences as a way to reinforce the important.

- **Practice transparency.** To reinforce both accountability and trust, deploy real-time team dashboards and other means of "seeing" the progress that teams are making. Such dashboards provide visibility into bottlenecks and blockades that will naturally occur over the life of a Program or Project as well, giving the team and the PMO more time to work the issues.

- **Mandate low overhead.** Create flatter organizations with fewer levels of management and hierarchy to increase visibility, simplify accountability, and accelerate decision making.

- **Institute fewer gates.** Minimize the number of forced "stops" or gates and other checkpoints that teams often insert into processes; ensure teams work *together* as they create deliverables or artifacts, so that those who would otherwise need the gate (time!) to review deliverables or artifacts do not need it (or need much less gate/time to conduct a final review).

Additional Benefits of Diversity Teaming

Establishing diverse and inclusive teams are their own reward, yielding benefits that allow our Program and Project teams to solve otherwise elusive problems. Beyond improved innovation, ideation, and leveraging different ways of thinking and solving problems, our boundary-spanning and cross-cultural teams also provide their parent organizations with benefits based on the ability to:

- Increase ideation, solutioning, testing, and support velocity by working across time zones in a *follow the sun* manner

- Similarly, reduce time-to-value by working around the sun

- Draw on lower-cost labor pools and expertise from multiple sites:

  o Acquire otherwise unavailable expertise

  o Enable sharing of expertise between Programs and Projects

  o Help reduce *brain drain* out of a single site or team

- Distribute, expose, and mitigate risks across a greater breadth of experience and insight

- Help our teams naturally expand their influence and capabilities across lines previously viewed as boundaries; our teams can establish global footprints while pursuing literally world-class excellence:

  o Establish a presence in multiple locations, which in turn can be grown and used as needs evolve globally as well as locally

  o Customize solutions to problems based on local needs

The financial and flexibility-derived benefits only reinforce our diverse teams' effectiveness and value.

Guiding Principles for Effective Teams and Workplaces

With our knowledge of organizational culture covered in Chapter 6, and our knowledge here around what it means to draw on that culture to create effective teams, consider the following Guiding Principles.

- Very few things worthwhile can be tackled effectively or completed solo; Programs and Projects are inclusive team sports, not individual efforts.

- Pursue and build diversity into every team by practicing **Diversity by Design**.

- Trust is the glue that binds diverse and inclusive teams; consider how (and how well) you are building that trust.

- Trust is also the glue that helps preserve teams over the long-term; high attrition often points to low trust.

- Transparency acts as a multiplier for accountability and builds respect if not empathy across teams.

- If a team does not have a singular or well-defined purpose organized around its goals or outcomes, the team is either too big or no longer required.

- Every human has biases; those who are unaware of their own biases will inadvertently damage relationships and reputations and in doing so negatively influence the tactical work climate and ultimately the overall organizational culture.

- Biases reflect the past; learn from the past but more importantly consider the facts today and the realities coming with the future.

- Committees and Boards (virtual or *v-teams*) facilitate matrixed relationships; use these matrixes to enable yet another way of strengthening relationships between different teams and up and down organizational hierarchies.

- Before building a team, understand the organization's top-level culture and each prospective team member's individual or lowest-level culture; work climate is the good stuff between the two levels or two slices of bread making up a sandwich.

- Like good team leadership, good team "follower-ship" is just as important.

- Reflective teams are effective teams; model Design Thinking through intentional and *regularly scheduled* feedback or back-brief sessions. Course correct based on lessons learned.

- Diverse perspectives give us our best shot at solving hard problems; look around and confirm you've got that shot.

Summary

This chapter built on the communications and culture foundations established in Chapters 5 and 6, respectively, to explore diversity by design and collaborative teaming. We explored the operational principles for effective and collaborative teaming, followed by a look at perspectives, often neglected biases, and the Diversity Paradox.

Organizing for role clarity and to achieve faster time-to-value, along with providing a view into non-innovation advantages of diversity teaming and Guiding Principles for effective teams and workplaces, concluded the chapter.

All of the Design Thinking techniques explored here and elsewhere are outlined in Appendix B, *Design Thinking Techniques*, starting on p. 196.

Case Study

The Harmony Program Director is curious about the role of diversity among the Program's committees, boards, and teams as a way of creating a more effective and collaborative place to work, and he is interested in your thoughts. He has asked you to answer a few ad hoc questions to fill gaps in his understanding of effective teaming.

Chapter 7 Questions

1.   In what ways would an otherwise qualified individual need to operate to promote an effective and collaborative team?

2.   What does the story of the circle, the rectangle, and the cylinder illustrate?

3.   Given that Design Thinking puts forth the notion that we should "Build to Think," why is Action Bias to be avoided?

4.   How is transparency related to accountability and in turn to trust?

See Appendix A starting on p. 187 for Case Study answers.

Chapter 8

Program and Project Planning

- *The Initiate Phase: The Charter, Stakeholders, and PMO*
- *The Define and Plan Phase: Creating Plans and Artifacts*
- *Applying Design Thinking to the Define and Plan Phase*
- *Getting Ready for Mobilization*
- *Guiding Principles for Building the PMO*
- *Guiding Principles for Creating Plans and Artifacts*
- *Chapter Summary and Case Study*

Planning aligns to both the Initiate and the Define and Plan phases of Program and Project Management (Figure 8.1).

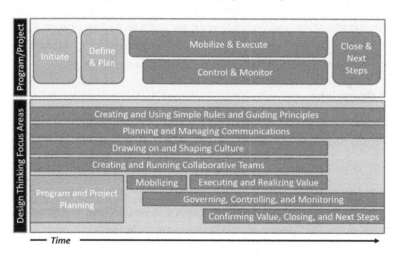

Figure 8.1 Start applying Design Thinking to Planning in the earliest days.

Despite our "build to think" Design Thinking technique that tells us we need to jump in and start building, a certain amount of planning is still necessary for successful delivery of a service, capability, or outcome; carefully applying Design Thinking to this work will help us get it done better and faster, however. Building on the basics of Chapter 3, this chapter walks us through applying Design Thinking to standing up the

PMO, thinking through the Perils we will encounter along the journey, establishing the various planning processes spanning Program and Project Management, and more. As a reminder, we have formatted these Design Thinking techniques in **bold** to help you spot them. Read more about each of these in Appendix B, *Design Thinking Techniques*, p. 196.

The Initiate Phase: The Charter, Stakeholders, and PMO

The first step in the Initiate Phase is to build the Program or Project Charter, a document that will be issued by the Program or Project initiator or Sponsor. The Charter documents the "high-level project description and boundaries, high-level requirements and risks," stakeholders, summarized milestones, key deliverables, success criteria, and preapproved financial resources (Project Management Institute, 2017) supporting the Program's or Project's business case. The Charter serves as the overall "starting point" for planning the rest of the work.

*The smartest thing we can do to create well-known or standardized documents such as a Program or Project Charter is to use a **Standardized Template**.*

Because the PMO has not yet been established, we will need to turn to another source for such templates. Consider the following:

- Look internally in the organization for previous Program or Project Charters that can serve as our template.
- Search across the net for a reasonable starting point (many sites offer good samples, including http://templatearchive.com)
- Enlist the help of a third party, such as a Systems Integrator.
- Worst-case, follow the Project Management Institute's (2017) detailed guidance as to the Table of Contents for a Charter, and create it from scratch.

Next, we need to identify all of the Stakeholders connected to the Program or Project. Create and use a **Stakeholder Map** to visually organize all of the roles or groups that have a stake or vested interest in the Program's or Project's solution and other intended outcomes (the stakeholder register serves many of the same purposes). Organize the Stakeholder Map around users, Sponsors, executive leaders, partners, and the various teams required to design, develop, test, deploy, and operate the solution being managed by the PMO.

---

*Use the **Stakeholder Map** to inform and develop the overall Program or Project Management Plan and its component plans.*

Finally, while not strictly a part of the Project Management Institute's guidance, for our purposes here we want to cover establishing the Program or Project Management Office (PMO). The PMO is the governance organization that provides program/project management support functions, templates, and guidance. Consider the following key decisions:

- Determine the type of PMO required, ranging from a low-touch Supportive PMO, to a Controlling PMO, to a high-touch Directive PMO; work with the initiator or Sponsor and the Program's or Project's earliest leaders and thinkers to work through a bit of **Brainstorming**, perform a **Culture Assessment**, and apply **Modular Thinking** to determine and start designing a best-fit PMO.

- Determine the most effective type of initial PMO leadership, ranging from charismatic or visionary to situational, transformational, servant, transactional, and others. In this case, the type of Program or Project will help drive the necessary initial leadership style; complex transformational Programs and Projects tend to benefit most from visionary and highly active leaders and change agents but in all cases benefit from transparent and empathetic leadership.

- The style of leadership needed to get things started may be very different from the leadership required later during execution. Align your PMO leadership strategy to your **Time Horizons**, considering the type of work being executed and the influence and oversight necessary to complete that work.

- Based on the type of PMO, create an organizational design leveraging the organization's past learnings, **Standardized**

> **Templates**, and the Project Management Institute's (2017) guidance.

- Staff the PMO's key roles with people who reflect the desired leadership and working style(s), starting with the Program Manager or Project Manager followed by Team Leaders, Workstream Leads, and others. As much as possible, allow leaders to create their own teams and staff their own roles. Consider **Cobb's Paradox and Matrix** to think through and evaluate a number of project management-specific areas that continue to show up as key reasons why Programs and Projects fail (see Chapter 10 and Figure 10.2, p. 157, for additional information).

- Also consider how you can **Increase Shared Identity** by finding and creating common threads or themes between these initial leadership roles and teams, together which will help set and shape the PMO's culture and influence work climates.

- Once the core of the PMO team is formed, do the work of establishing the PMO's **Simple Rules** (the Who, What, and When that describes the team). See Chapter 4, p. 62, for more on thinking through and creating these Rules.

- Finally, create the PMO's **Guiding Principles** (the How), a sampling of which are provided at the end of this chapter.

The PMO and its leaders go a long way towards establishing a healthy and constructive work environment. But it is important to remember that PMO leadership does not replace the tone set by an organization's executive team.

Leaders model behaviors and through this modeling effectively dictate which behaviors are acceptable and which are not acceptable (Graziano, 2019).

Be sure to **Broadly Understand** the overall organization's executive leadership tone under which the PMO will operate.

The Define and Plan Phase: Creating Plans and Artifacts

As we saw in Chapter 3, we need to plan for, verify, and create a great number of artifacts that we will then use to manage our Program's or Project's work. The Project Management Institute (2017) refers to this effort as the Planning process group, and we have expanded this process group a bit to also include "defining" certain foundational artifacts.

The list below reflects the Program-level Plans and artifacts we must build that together form the Program Management Plan. Even if we are not running a Program per se, these five areas are nonetheless super important to think through and plan for:

- **Strategy Management Plan,** which includes the Program Roadmap illustrating how the Program fits into the organization's broader Portfolio of Programs, Projects, and Initiatives.

- **Benefits Management Plan,** which includes the Benefits Realization Plan (comprised of the Benefits Register and the analysis, planning, and delivery of those benefits) and the Transition and Sustainment Plan detailing how the benefits derived from the Program will be transitioned to the organization and sustained post-Program.

- **Stakeholder Engagement Management Plan,** which includes the Stakeholder Engagement Plan comprised of the Stakeholder Map and processes for maintaining and managing stakeholder engagement.

- **Program Life Cycle Management Plan,** which includes a description and timeline of the high-level Program phases, the set of Program-level summarized plans, the master schedule, and sometimes the various Component Project Management Plans underpinning the Program.

- **Program Governance Plan,** which includes the Governance Roles and Responsibilities matrix, the structure and makeup of the various Governance Bodies, the Governance Communications Plan (comprising cadences for meetings, important stage gates, Program/Project performance reviews, and approval-to-proceed processes), along with Simple Rules, Guiding Principles, other decision-making norms, and escalation processes; governance is explored in more detail in Chapter 11.

Beyond these Program-level plans and artifacts, we also need to build a great number of plans and artifacts for every Component Project that "rolls up" to the Program. These plans and artifacts include:

- The **Project Management Plan**, an umbrella comprised of a:
  - Scope Management Plan
  - Project Schedule and its visual corollary the Gantt Chart, a tactical Work Breakdown Structure (WBS), and task sequences and durations
  - Project Cost and Budget Management Plan
  - Quality Management Plan
  - Resource Management Plan
  - Communications Plan
  - Risk Management Plan
  - Procurement Management Plan
  - Stakeholder Engagement Plan

- The **Project Change Control** process each team will use to make and manage changes to their respective Component Project

- The **Business Change Management Plan** and related **Training Plans** necessary to help users learn the new systems and processes introduced through each Project

- The **IT Change Management Plan**, in cases where the IT team itself will need to learn new skills as the result of a Project

- The initial basics of a **Data Migration Plan**

- The initial basics of a **Technical Integration Plan**

- The **Deliverables Review** process for Plans, artifacts, documents, and other outcomes that the Project team will create along the journey

Applying Design Thinking to the Define and Plan Phase

Each Project Management Plan acts as a tactical *playbook* for its respective Project. Each Plan has a unique set of users for whom the Plan is built, but the Plans themselves reflect well-known needs and a great amount of consistency. Thus, each Plan can be designed in a repeatable low-effort manner:

- To build all of our Plans and artifacts, start first with a set of **Standardized Templates**, one for each plan (as we did for developing the Program or Project Charter).
- Effective templates will help to ensure we do not miss anything mandatory or foundational.
- The best templates are **Modular**, too, which will help us move quickly through the "build" process by reusing structures or content between documents.

Next, consider and apply the following Design Thinking techniques to each plan or artifact:

- **Align Strategy to Time Horizons.** As we develop roadmaps, schedules, and other time-oriented strategic artifacts, think about the "now" (real-time), the short-term, and the long-term. We need to align our strategy with these time horizons, recognizing that our long-term and mid-term visions must be prioritized as much as our short-term vision if they are to be realized.

- **Balance the Accidental with the Essential.** As we create potentially complex documents, consider the complexity that is necessary vs the complexity that can be removed. Similar to **Minimalism**, create as *lightweight* an artifact as possible without losing the artifact's intention or its value to users.

- Consider the **Feedback Loops** that need to be implemented around each artifact to help us apply learnings from prototyping, iterating, testing, and other Design Thinking activities.

Another key benefit of Design Thinking is the notion of looping back or "looping to apply learnings."

- During testing or **Piloting** of a plan or artifact, and again after the final solution has been formally deployed, consider how **Gamification** might be used to create yet another **Feedback Loop** or drive desired changes in behavior including broader and faster adoption.

- In the same way, pay attention to the **Silent Design** efforts in play once our plans, processes, and artifacts are actually in use. For example, learn from users and gather feedback by observing the changes they make to their artifacts, how they might be "marked up" or modified to be more effective, and how users work around areas with which they are unhappy.

---

*The idea behind tracking **Silent Design** is to reactively funnel learnings back into a solution or artifact. Be proactive as well; ask users what needs to be done differently to make the solutions or artifacts we give them more usable or user-centric.*

- **Increase Shared Identity.** As we create Project-specific processes and documents, build on the work started when the PMO was established and create opportunities for shared experiences (team meals, after-work events, morning coffee cadences, and so on). Work to create common threads or connections between new people/teams and in-place people and teams. These threads and connections help replace "differences" with similarities, all of which are useful to create and sustain shared visions, drive stronger relationships and collaboration, and further shape a team's work climate and an organization's culture.

- Employ **Modular Thinking and Building.** In the name of reusability and to keep artifact/document maintenance cycles low, create modular components (so standard components or modules can be shared and reused between documents or recombined to create new artifacts that Stakeholders might request in the future).

- Prior to creating Program and Project Plans and other artifacts, conduct a bit of **Empathy Mapping** or perform a lightweight **Persona Analysis** of its users and readers. Doing so makes it easier to know and therefore consistently write to or create for the specific people who will use the artifacts.

- When it comes time to plan for Training, again use the **Persona Analysis** process to organize users logically. Consider cultural attributes that might drive a certain training format or style (i.e. informal Knowledge Transfer sessions vs more formal Classroom-based education sessions vs self-service job aids and urgent-care support for real-time assistance.

- To develop Risk Management Plans and similar what-if artifacts, perform a **CARMA Analysis** to wade through and compare risk-influenced options, and use the **Premortem** approach to think ahead as to risks that might be realized, why and how they might be realized, and mitigation strategies useful in thwarting risk realization. Group-based premortems can also be fantastic for helping teams see and discuss biases in their thinking (i.e. confirmation bias or group think).

- Finally, to help determine the viability of our solutions, plans, processes, and artifacts, collect **User Engagement Metrics** to track how they are used and how well our users think we have engaged them.

The list above is not exhaustive; you will surely find other techniques useful. Again, consider the Design Thinking techniques and approaches shared in Appendix B, *Design Thinking Techniques*.

Getting Ready for Mobilization

With our Plans and key artifacts in place, we need to turn our attention to the many remaining "readiness" tasks we must tackle as part of the upcoming Mobilization phase. In general, we need to think through:

- Verifying active sponsorship and executive engagement
- Hiring remaining key roles
- Retaining our valuable hires! (Anitha & Begum, 2016)
- Getting everyone ready or Mobilized
- Getting each team to the Starting Line
- Ensuring each team creates and socializes its Simple Rules and Guiding Principles

- Ensuring every team member has the tools and other resources they need to execute.

Chapter 9, *Mobilization*, p. 133, goes into each of these areas in detail, organized around the Perils we discussed previously in Chapter 1.

Guiding Principles for Building the PMO

As the first team built, the PMO plays a key role in setting the stage well for a successful Program or Project. Consider the following Guiding Principles:

- The Program (or Project) Charter gives the PMO its authority; understand where these lines are drawn.

- The PMO will set the leadership and cultural tone for the Program or Project; therefore, design and staff the PMO with care.

- A PMO delivers business outcomes and benefits; maintain this focus by establishing and measuring Key Performance Indicators.

- The style of Leadership to get us started will probably not be the style of Leadership that gets us through the long term; think through what is needed from a leadership perspective and when it is needed.

- To increase the odds of a team's success and to increase leader accountability and buy-in, as much as possible allow leaders to staff their teams.

- Few issues can taint or crush a Program or Project worse than ethical leadership missteps and outright moral failure; think through and background check your leaders carefully.

- While initiative can be modeled or taught, a track record of initiative is priceless; look for evidence of drive and a "get-it-done" or *hungry* attitude.

- Consider the mantra "Hire for attitude and train for skills," realizing that a certain amount of skill is still required in many cases.

- Look for and onboard "learn-it-all" and "listen-to-it-all" people rather than "know-it-all" people; the latter simply don't...

- Experienced resources are not necessarily the most qualified resources (if at all); experience is but one dimension of qualification.

- Employ modular organizational designs to facilitate resource sharing and reusability.

- Employ lightweight governance until a heavier hand is needed.

- Know yourself—your team, Project, Program, or organization— through a Simple Rules exercise.

- Consider culture ramifications before deciding on the type of PMO to employ, and again before staffing the PMO.

- If you are standing up a *Supporting PMO* model, consider third party providers when the methodology, tools, and templates they bring with them are specifically designed for the type of Program or Project they're asked to implement.

- When inevitable issues arise, focus on the issues and underlying behaviors, not the person.

- Transparent and empathetic leadership goes a long way towards building and retaining a team of the best and brightest (Tyler, 2019); most everyone realizes that no one is perfect. Model humility and a **Growth Mindset**.

Guiding Principles for Creating Plans and Artifacts

We reviewed a breadth of Design Thinking techniques for quickly creating usable Plans and artifacts.

- Understand each artifact's users or user community and do your homework to reflect their needs.

- Accelerate your progress and avoid key content misses through **Standardized Templates**.

- Focus first on a plan's or artifact's Table of Contents; with the right content organization, the content itself becomes easier to create, edit, and manage.

- Employ **Co-Innovation** to create documents and other artifacts side-by-side with those who will use them.

- Socialize artifacts early and request feedback on the Table of Contents, format, style, and content often.

- Content is King; focus on delivering the vital "what" of plans, deliverables, artifacts, and other work products.

- Focus on usability or consumability as well as content; create and use meaningful figures and pictures.

- Be consistent across plans, artifacts, and other documents; use the same format, fonts, application of bold/highlights, and color-coding until there is good reason to do something differently.

- Spell out and explain all acronyms and terms incorporated into high-touch or high-use plans, artifacts, and other documents; new users are commonly added to Programs and Projects over time, making it impossible to assume a shared vocabulary.

- Remember to accommodate the **Rule of Threes** which suggests it takes three iterations to really get something right.

- Build **Feedback Loops** into the document creation and review process; consider **Gamification** and drawing on **Silent Design**; the more our documents are socialized and used, the more opportunities we have to remediate gaps or other shortcomings.

- Store all documents in a secured yet easily accessible document management or collaboration system where they can be edited in place, version-controlled, audited, regularly backed up, and maintained.

- Build time into the Project Plan or calendar to refresh key plans and living artifacts at least quarterly; if the time is not set aside, the refresh will likely never occur.

Summary

This chapter introduced the Initiate phase followed by the Define and Plan phase. We looked at applying a great number of Design Thinking techniques to building our Program or Project Charter, Stakeholder Map, the PMO, and a host of plans and artifacts. All of this planning sets the stage for Mobilization. We concluded Chapter 8 with a set of Guiding Principles for Building the PMO and for building our Plans and Artifacts.

All of the Design Thinking techniques explored here and elsewhere are outlined in Appendix B, *Design Thinking Techniques*, starting on p. 196.

Case Study

You have been asked to help work through some of the first steps related to the Initiate and the Define and Plan phases. As you know, the Harmony Program is a multi-year transformation effort comprised of several Component Projects. Harmony's stakeholders have several questions that need to get answered related to Program and Project planning.

Chapter 8 Questions

1. What document serves as the overall "starting point" and key foundational document you should read through first, and from where does it come?

2. Which Design Thinking techniques might be useful in determining the type of PMO to create?

3. Which Design Thinking technique serves as a universal starting point for creating repeatable and consistent documents?

4. With so many Plans and other artifacts to create, which Design Thinking techniques can we use to help us ensure we understand our audience's or users' needs?

See Appendix A starting on p. 187 for Case Study answers.

Chapter 9

Mobilizing for Effectiveness

o   *Thinking through the Remaining Perils*
o   *Staffing, Organizing, and Onboarding*
o   *Validating and Improving Capabilities*
o   *Funding, Budgets, and Contracts*
o   *Ensuring Active and Visible Sponsorship*
o   *Readying for Change*
o   *Removing remaining Efficacy Blockers*
o   *Guiding Principles for Effective Mobilization*
o   *Chapter Summary and Case Study*

Mobilization, or *getting ready to execute*, is the topic of this chapter (see Figure 9.1). We will cover a number a number of readiness areas including working through several remaining Perils first outlined in Chapter 1. For each Peril, we will consider Design Thinking techniques shown to be useful in mitigating, circumventing, or eliminating them.

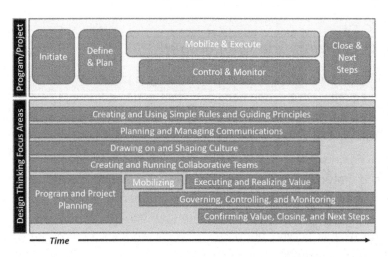

Figure 9.1 Mobilizing people and teams is a critical Design Thinking focus area.

Thinking through the Remaining Perils

With the work of the Initiate and the Define and Plan phases behind us, we need to mobilize our people and our teams. Mobilizing is the first step in the long journey of Program or Project execution. Here in Chapter 9, we cover what it means to mobilize and get ahead of the following Perils:

- Avoiding the **Staffing Sand Trap** by staffing our teams, organizing the work, and onboarding team members

- Crossing the **Capabilities Chasms** by validating and improving team capabilities and overall readiness

- Crossing the **Budget Bridges** and avoiding **Contracting Mudslides** by validating our paperwork is in order and in place

- Managing the **Sponsorship Volcano** by ensuring active and persistently visible Sponsorship

- Navigating the inevitable **Change Waves** by ensuring our teams are prepared for the Changes they will face

- Shutting down any remaining **Efficacy Bandits** and other blockers that could hurt our chances of getting the hard work done.

Given its *critical path* importance, let us turn to staffing first.

Staffing, Organizing, and Onboarding

Staffing is about hiring. Unfortunately, hiring people is too often an exercise in tradeoffs. On the one hand, we want and need people who are not only experienced but qualified to do the work (experience is an important aspect of qualification, but it's not everything).

On the other hand, we also need to hire culturally and emotionally intelligent and mature people who possess the attitude and abilities to navigate ambiguity, work effectively despite culture and other differences, and come alongside fellow team members to help ensure everyone doesn't just survive but does their best work on the Program's or Project's journey together (see Figure 9.2).

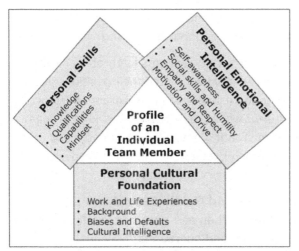

Figure 9.2 Every team member is broadly influenced in three ways.

Employ **Shadowing** and situation-specific team **Collaboration** to help mature or up-level individuals and teams.

For key leadership roles, avoid making staffing tradeoffs; you need the full package. In other cases, you may be able to train or develop team members to "create" the full package over time.

Organizing the Work

Typically, we staff for specific roles or positions in an organization. But in the early days of a Program or Project, we have some flexibility simply because the organization itself is more flexible. We need to think about our people and the organizational structure together.

- How can our people help us create a capability-rich organization?

- How might we **Ideate or Innovate** to fit super talented individuals we run across into our organization despite the lack of perfect-fit roles? To what extent can we create specific roles for specific high-performing people?

- How should we organize the work we need to complete? Are there natural team boundaries between various business and IT organizations that we can leverage? Apply a **Design Mindset** and **Brainstorming** to organizational structuring.

- If we are bringing in a third-party systems integrator or software implementation partner, should we match their positions like-for-like with similarly aligned positions on our Program or Project team? Called *two-in-a-box* or *matched pairs*, this kind of team structure lends itself to creating naturally accountable and collaborative workstreams or teams (at the risk of imperfect work balances; be sure the work can be and is distributed).

- What set of **Simple Rules and Guiding Principles** are needed to identify the Who, What, When and How that together describe the organization's structure and operations?

Onboarding Team Members

Once hired for the Program or Project, team members need to be *onboarded* or brought aboard. Effective onboarding takes planning and much preparation. And it is incredibly important to become good at it.

Preparing for inevitable attrition or long-term illnesses... addressing inadequate qualifications, capabilities, or culture fit... and planning for the team's future needs dictates that we become experts at onboarding new people quickly and efficiently.

How might we smoothly transition a new team member into our Program or Project at different phases? What level of detail should we include in our onboarding package shared with every team member? For starters, consider the **Day in the Life** of a new team member... think through what they will face and what they will need in those early days and weeks. Apply **Minimalism** to create the onboarding package, pulling together and sharing the following for starters:

- The Program's or Project's vision and problem being solved

- A high-level synopsis of the overall Scope of Work

- A high-level Program roadmap or schedule of key milestones

- The list of key work products to be created, including a description of the solution, deliverables, and artifacts

- The **Stakeholder Map, Decision Authority Map,** and pertinent history or other details

- Site logistics including access and security considerations and key contact information

- Work standards and collaboration tools (including access to those tools and basic "How to Use..." guidance)

- A high-level view of the implementation methodology

- A primer on communication norms and expectations

Other matters need to be considered as well, particularly if there is a *transition process* exists between outgoing and incoming personnel.

- Allow transition time between the new team member onboarding and a person who is exiting that role. Consider **Shadowing** or using the **Day in the Life** technique.

- Consider using the **Buddy System** where a new team member is paired with a veteran team member for a period of time (such as the first month after hiring) to help answer early questions, provide background data, and allow the new person the chance to ease into their new role and culture.

- Allow the new team member to observe, work with, or otherwise **Shadow** not just another Program or Project team member but also one of the Program's or Project's business users. Doing so will afford another connection point into the organization while developing empathy for the very community who will be affected by the work of the Program or Project.

Validating and Improving Capabilities

Each team members brings a set of capabilities to the Program or Project team. Some of these capabilities might be very specialized (such as deep technical skills in a particular area). Other capabilities might be much more general or difficult to quantify (such as the ability to work effectively in the midst of ambiguity, or the ability to partner and collaborate exceptionally well with others).

Regardless, capabilities serve as a "bridge" spanning numerous chasms or cliffs on our Program or Project roadmap. It is important that our teams reflect the breadth of capabilities necessary to survive the journey; fortunately, not everyone needs every skill. If we have many of the same gaps, do we have an opportunity to implement a **Scaling for Effectiveness** technique?

The inability of a team to execute the work for which it is responsible will slow the work down, potentially drive lop-sided team obligations and burnout, affect the schedule, and burden the broader organization.

Capabilities reflect a certain maturity level, too, akin to a combination of experience and process diligence or formality. An immature capability would be delivered in an ad hoc fashion, whereas a more mature capability would reflect defined steps and metrics. As we hire and develop our teams, we need to consider each member's current capabilities and maturity level. In some cases, beyond **Shadowing** and mentoring and formal training, we might need to build a readiness plan to improve those capabilities or the maturity level by which they're delivered. In other cases, **Gamification** and similar techniques could help drive engagement and reinforce new behaviors.

Funding, Budgets, and Contracts

Programs and Projects comprise a tremendous amount of paperwork before and during execution. The work must be funded and approved, budgets need to be developed and managed, and resources need to be contracted or licensed.

- Is an initial Budget set forth in the Program or Project Charter? Is it enough? Are budget inflection points known?

- Are there contingency funds available if we need them? How do we access those funds? Has our organization's leadership team or the Steering Committee approved additional spending? Is that additional spending contingent upon **Aligning our Strategy** (to a particular) **Time Horizon**?

- How and when will financial status be tracked? For the largest Programs, should we consider drawing up a finance-specific **Persona** and related **Customer Journey Map**?

- Have the Contracts and Licensing been reviewed by Procurement and Legal? Are we actually licensed correctly to develop and deploy what we intend to develop and deploy? Do we need any additional or separate subscriptions or related paperwork done?

- Are all contracts signed and executed? What about contracts or licensing needs we might have with partners or other third parties? Should we execute a **Premortem** to help us think through potential licensing and contracting "what if..." issues?

There are also specific circumstances or issues that need to be considered proactively.

- Is there funding available to "backfill" people who have left standard roles to help deliver a role on the Program or Project? Most roles in a large transformation are full-time after all, making it impractical for team members to wear two hats or work part-time on old roles and their new Program/Project role.

- Do we have a training and travel budget for our team members?

- Do we have dependencies on other in-flight Programs and Projects that might impact our budget or our schedule? Do we have dependencies in a contract that still needs to be addressed?

Ensuring Active and Visible Sponsorship

Active sponsorship must start on *Day One*, typically with the team that created and published the Charter, and it must continue through Program or Project Close.

A lack of strong sponsorship is still cited as a top reason explaining Program and Project failures; for complex and protracted endeavors, managing Sponsor engagement is that much more critical.

The Sponsor crafts and shares the strategic vision, working at the executive stakeholder level to bring everyone along. This vision must be shared with all stakeholders and key team members alike, and includes:

- What business problems are we trying to solve?
- What is our strategy for solving those problems?
- What does success look like, and how will we measure it?
- How will we be different tomorrow than we are today, and why is that difference important?
- Are all stakeholders identified in the stakeholder register and **Stakeholder Map**? Has the map been updated regularly?
- Are all stakeholders aligned around the vision? Is there an opportunity to **Increase Shared Identity**?
- In what ways have **Feedback Loops** been employed to funnel thoughts and ideas back up to the Sponsor and other Stakeholders?

Everyone needs to know that the Program or Project work is supported at the highest levels. Too many times the executive team fails to provide clear vision, and this lack of clarity muddles and confounds its way throughout an organization.

Sponsors resemble "coaches" in that they exert influence within an organization to get everyone moving towards the same destination. We need our coach to remain active and visible! And when the Program or Project inevitably runs into problems, we need our coach ready to step in and lead from the front with confidence, fully equipped with the data needed to make the decisions necessary to get things back on track.

Readying for Change

When implementing Programs and Projects, change comes in several flavors. Arguably the most important is the change that the Business will need to prepare for as the Program or Project delivers value in the form of a delivered solution, new systems, and new business processes.

Business Change Management

Business change management is as much about driving sound business changes as it is about staying engaged. Business Sponsors and other business leaders need to have the respect of their organizations to make tough decisions and trade-offs throughout the implementation's journey. They must also understand the organization's pain, drive the kind of change that remedies that pain, and help the organization absorb that change. Questions along the journey include:

- As the Program or Project marches on, how are the overarching business objectives being clearly articulated and reinforced across the business and its people? Is there an opportunity to **Co-Innovate**?

- How strong is the Executive team's alignment with the Program or Project? What about Board alignment?

- What have we done to help our non-Business team members **Broadly Understand** and **Empathize** with our users? Do we have an **Empathy Map** upon which to draw?

- Are there Program or higher-level forthcoming changes (think "mergers and acquisitions or divestitures") that could impact the work currently in progress? What other systems or processes will be impacted by the new system?

- Are there fundamental culture implications that would benefit from **Culture Assessments** or better understanding **Cultural Intelligence**?

- What should the Program or Project team, working with the Business, design into training programs, business readiness, and other change adoption efforts? Would a **Day in the Life Analysis** help set the stage?

- Does each Functional Team represented in the Program or Project have the organizational clout and vision to make tough trade-offs or tie-breakers? Are they empowered to make decisions at their business or process level? Does everyone have a shared understanding of the **Definition of the Problem(s)**?

- Similarly, have we thought about the various business teams or divisions, and their hierarchy, i.e. who "wins" process decision approvals?

- Do we have the best and right Subject Matter Experts (SMEs)? How should our **Design Mindset** be engaged or shifted to evolve our SMEs into "Solution Champions" or "Change Champions"?

- How do we measure and reward our business SMEs to drive the right values and motivation? Are we asking our people to work against an outdated set of rules, regulations, or irrelevant delivery processes? (Berman, 2006)? Beyond talk, do we actually operate under the belief that people will work harder *and* be more fulfilled when they're valued?

- In terms of SME representation, do we have a clear sense of the **Personas** they can represent on behalf of the Program or Project?

- In terms of SME staffing, do we have the right combination of veterans (with deep experience and past battle scars) and less senior team members (with fewer preconceived notions who might help us see and **Ideate** differently)?

- In terms of SME bandwidth, have we organized for backfills (so our SMEs can focus exclusively on the Program or Project rather than on their old job PLUS their demanding new job)?

- Finally, what are we doing to create and drive an effective Adoption and Change Management (ACM) strategy? Have we created a strong ACM team? Does our ACM team or its leads have a track record of helping teams and customers realize solution benefits in previous (and similarly complex) Programs and Projects? Are we using **Postmortems**, **Retrospectives**, and other lessons learned from those past efforts?

Program or Project Change Control

Because Program and Project scopes rarely remain static, it is necessary to think ahead as to how proposed changes will be opened, documented, reviewed, dispositioned, tracked, and closed:

- Is the change considered necessary to the successful outcome of the Program or Project? If so, what has changed or why was the proposed change "missed" or unnecessary until now? Has our understanding of the **Customer Journey Map** changed?

- Is an alternative solution possible? Should we engage in some **Divergent Thinking** or employ **Minimalism** in the short term (or longer)? Do we need to perform **Rapid Prototyping** of the change or of the alternative before we make our decision?

- What is the required effort (cost/hours) and timeline (schedule) for thinking through and implementing the change? Are there any **Time Pacing** implications to consider?

- What are the implications if the change is rejected (by the PMO or business team or other affected party)? In that case, what is the escalation path to make the final decision? Does our **Stakeholder Map** reflect this escalation path?

Managing IT Team Changes

A final important type of change affects the IT team. Just as the business must prepare for changes in its processes, so too must the IT team prepare for changes in what it runs, how it operates, and so on. Changes could be as fundamental as those related to new (traditional or cloud-based) infrastructure, from network and storage to servers (compute) and storage systems. Changes might include new database systems and integration solutions to applications, too. All of these technologies will require new methods and processes for operating, updating, upgrading, patching, and generally maintaining.

To prepare for these changes, document the current and the future technology stacks, identify the "deltas" between the two stacks, and:

- Think about the **Adjacent Spaces** a team will need to learn and master. What can be leveraged in the "current" spaces to ease the transition to the adjacent spaces?

- Should we be thinking through or preparing for a more specific **Time Horizon**?

- Are our changes following a natural **Inverse Power Law**, or will we overwhelm the team with too many major changes at once (for example)?

- Consider what the team will still have to continue to manage out of the old stack; **Minimize the Variables**.

- If many teams are affected in similar ways, consider a "franchise" approach to introducing and preparing for the change as explained in **Scaling for Effectiveness** (p. 205); to push out smaller changes, a **Shadowing** approach might be useful.

Removing remaining Efficacy Blockers

Before we move to Chapter 10 and core Program and Project execution, we need to think through any remaining conditions or blockers that could affect a team's ability to do its work. We call these "efficacy blockers," where the notion of efficacy is linked to getting hard things done. Anything that gets in the way of getting hard things done needs to be mitigated or eliminated!

Look to an organization's track record of past successes and failures to understand and prioritize the efficacy blockers it probably still faces today.

- More than half of all transformational Programs and Projects never even finish, and some research puts this number at closer to 80%. What are we doing better and differently to beat those odds?

- Are we paying attention to and learning from **Cobb's Paradox** which tells us we need strong Project Managers and standardized project management processes (among other findings)?

- Do we have a proven track record of getting hard things done? Do we consistently reach the Finish Line? Why or why not?

- Do our team leaders find a way to navigate through ambiguity, risks, and issues? Do they truly lead? Or have we needed "Superman" and "Superwoman" in the past to lead us through ambiguity to victory?

- Do our teams collaborate and communicate effectively? How are we measuring the notion of effectiveness?

- Do we understand dependencies we have on other Programs, Projects, Portfolios, or Initiatives?

- Have we thought recently about our leadership team and how it might be time for a change in personnel, style, or both?

- Are we thinking with the end in mind? Specifically, are we thinking through *Deployment Strategies* (and backing that thinking into how our current workstreams need to plan their work or change their structures)?

Consider the following Design Thinking techniques:

- Each team needs to run through a team-specific **Premortem** exercise. What might happen in the future to derail our Program or Project, and therefore what steps should we take to avoid that future? How can the **Five Why's** help us explore an unclear future?

- Do we have a complete set of **Guiding Principles** to help us quickly think through future decisions and future unknowns?

- To what extent should we setup a regular cadence to think through and **Assess our Culture** as it changes a person at a time over time?

- Are we considering **Time Horizons**, and paying particular attention to the oft-ignored middle or mid-term Time Horizon?

- How might we ensure our Diverse-by-Design teams engage in healthy communication and **Collaboration**?

With our Perils properly mitigated or eliminated for the time being, we've essentially helped our people and our Teams finally get to the Starting Line. Let the Program or Project begin!

Guiding Principles for Effective Mobilization

Consider the following guidance for successfully mobilizing our people, our teams, and our stakeholder and sponsor support structure.

- As part of mobilizing, each team must do the work of brainstorming, identifying, codifying, publishing, and living by their Simple Rules and Guiding Principles.

- Staffing decisions are often the most important of all decisions; do your homework, check your references, and be willing to admit (and act on) hiring mistakes quickly.

- Do not confuse misguided compassion with empathy; team members without the right capabilities and attitudes serving in the wrong roles will eventually poison the team's health.

- For every role, understand not only the core capabilities needed by a person to be successful in that role, but the maturity and experience level needed as well.

- For every team member, assess and then create a Development Plan that includes improving their personal Skills, personal Emotional Intelligence, and teachable aspects of their personal Cultural Foundation (including training on biases and Cultural Intelligence).

- When mobilizing, staffing, and preparing, consider when to apply marathon "long-term" thinking vs sprint "short-term" thinking, and recognize when it is time to change that thinking.

Remember that the "long pole" for many endeavors lies in the mundane paperwork and other administrative tasks that have to get gone; give the important mundane tasks the same attention you give the important yet more interesting tasks.

- For large packaged software implementations, during Mobilization drive a Configure vs Customize mentality across the whole of the PMO and stakeholder community; ensure every team member understands and embraces the differences between packaged solution implementation and greenfield custom development.

- Managing "change" is at the core of every Program or Project; instill this fact early, empathize deeply, and help minimize the pain of change.

- Never underestimate the power of active and visible sponsorship; pursue and build relationships with the Sponsor and settle for nothing less than active and visible engagement.

- Completing a Program or Project is more than getting everyone to the Finish Line together; a successful Program or Project starts with getting the core team ready and mobilized at the Starting Line.

Summary

This chapter presented the varied tasks comprising mobilization. From staffing and validating team capabilities to addressing the paperwork of funding and budgets and contracts, mobilization is about getting ready to execute. We looked at several other critical areas including sponsorship and change readiness before concluding with a discussion around efficacy blockers. In the next chapter, we will finally take those first steps into Execution!

Case Study

The FAST leadership team and the core Harmony Program team need assurances that the Program is ready to move into the Execute phase. Too many "readiness" issues have surfaced recently, making people nervous. The Program Director has requested your help assessing the team's readiness and other important aspects of Mobilizing.

All of the Design Thinking techniques explored here and elsewhere are outlined in Appendix B, *Design Thinking Techniques*, starting on p. 196.

Chapter 9 Questions

1. The Program team will surely face many Perils along the way. Which ones did we cover in this chapter related specifically to mobilization and readiness?

2. To ensure the Program team has been "onboarded" in a consistent kind of way, what types of information should comprise the Onboarding Package?

3. What are the three big areas of "Change Readiness" to be validated?

4. How would you explain the notion of "efficacy blockers" and in particular what Cobb's Paradox tells us about Program and Project Management?

See Appendix A starting on p. 187 for Case Study answers.

PART III

Executing at Speed

Chapter 10

Executing and Realizing Value

- *The Execute Phase*
- *Validating our Path through the Discovery Exercise*
- *Execution Processes*
- *Parallel Component Projects*
- *Efficacy and Effectiveness*
- *Executing to Think*
- *Guiding Principles for Execution and Realizing Value*
- *Chapter Summary and Case Study*

In Chapter 10, we apply Design Thinking to the real work of executing a Program or Project and realizing value from all that effort. This chapter builds on the foundation basics (the "what" of Program and Project Management) shared in Chapter 3; here in Chapter 10 we answer the question "How do I apply Design Thinking to execution?"

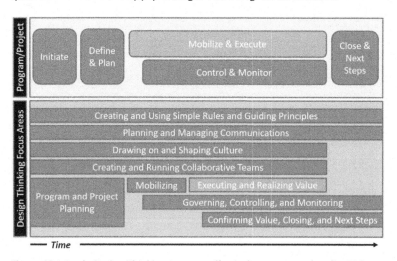

Figure 10.1 Apply Design Thinking to more effectively execute and realize Value.

The Execute Phase

So here we are, mobilized and armed with a Scope of Work, a set of requirements, a schedule, a team of ready and capable professionals dedicated to this specific endeavor, and more. We are at the place where "the rubber first meets the road," the Starting Line. The Execute phase brings together all of the resources required to implement the Program and/or Project Management plan(s), and includes the following execution activities:

- Hold any final *Discovery* workshops needed to understand the Scope of Work

- Create and manage the development of work products and other deliverables as identified in the Scope of Work

- Review and begin prioritizing requested changes

- Implement approved requests for change

- Apply corrective actions, course-correcting as necessary to ensure our work products meet our standards, timelines, budget commitments, and other guidelines or constraints

- Proactively think through and update the risk management plan as new risks are identified or realized

- Reactively address project issues (*realized risks*) as needed

- Gather work performance information

Through all of this, our mantra needs to "make progress and deliver." However, our first step necessitates stepping back and validating we understand the problem(s), our solution(s), and our plans.

Validating our Path through the Discovery Exercise

Working through a brief Discovery exercise helps us transition into Execution. To be clear, Discovery repeats or potentially iterates on some of the work previously completed when we created and refined the Scope of Work.

The key is to simply walk through the Discovery exercise before we formally start executing. Why? Because Discovery:

- Confirms our understanding of Requirements and therefore the Scope of Work before we pour our energy and resources into delivery; misunderstood or incomplete requirements lead to poor solution decisions, which in turn requires revisiting Scope, revising designs, and slowing everything down at great expense

- Forces us to revalidate the problems that triggered the Program's or Project's need in the first place

- Forces us to revisit the solution we intend to design, development, and deploy to solve those problems

- Helps us get more of the team on the same page (the later Discovery is done, presumably the more hiring we've completed)

- Serves as a "soft" start as we work through our collaboration, knowledge management, communication, and other processes before we commence on the larger effort.

Discovery inspired through Design Thinking (Herold, et al, 2019) follows several familiar steps below. Our Design Thinking techniques are highlighted in **bold text** as usual (refer to Appendix B, *Design Thinking Techniques*, starting on p. 196 for additional detail and other ideas):

1. Understand and Empathize

    o Seek to **Broadly Understand** by interviewing and interacting with the stakeholders and users tied to the Program or Project. Encourage **Story Telling** to explore and confirm general needs and the worst pain paints.

    o **Shadow** or run through a "**Day in the Life**" of key users to better understand their processes, pain points, and challenges.

    o Review current process flows and other available artifacts used today by the users.

2. Define the Problem

    o Identify the roles and **Personas** of each user community, including the objectives of each role. Be sure to understand their specific **Customer Journey Map**.

- o Document the specific decisions that users are required to complete for each task.

- o Continue documenting and refining your understanding of the problems and user's processes, pain points, and challenges, and **Define the Problem**.

3. Ideate

- o Prepare for ideation by completing any necessary pre-work; review outcomes from interviews and analysis; identify **Edge Cases** and other unique scenarios or features; determine where more discussion may be required; plan how to gather that additional information or features; and above all, embrace a solution-focused **Design Mindset**.

- o Identify relevant team members and assemble with them.

- o Put the current and planned solutions on the "shelf" (so they do not overtly influence or otherwise bias our ideation process) and run a **Hackathon** to explore and ideate.

- o Discuss the problems and put forth potential solutions, document ideas, whiteboard scenarios and processes, review concepts, and simulate test scenarios. Consider where we might want to **Backport into the Past**.

- o Make the design process interactive. Bring in other team members and users as necessary to think through new ideas. Consider opportunities to **Co-Innovate** side-by-side.

4. Mock-up and Prototype

- o At the earliest stages, create a **Mock-Up** (a very "light" prototype) of a conceptual solution or design. This can be achieved by drawing out screens or wireframes, using "sticky notes" or simple fish bone and process diagrams, and drawing up sample reports or other outcomes using Microsoft PowerPoint, Word, or Excel. Stay lightweight.

- o Consider to what extent the mock-up directionally aligns to the proposed Solution.

    - If too much complexity found its way in, consider **Backward Invention** and **Minimalism**.

- If there is good alignment between the planned solution or design and our ideation exercise and **Mock-Up**, end the Discovery exercise and proceed with Execution.

- If the team is seeing new opportunities or solutions to the problems, continue Discovery by returning back to Ideation or moving forward with prototyping (outlined next)

o Identify one or a few Use Cases or scenarios to **Prototype**

o **Prototype**, or "build to think" by creating a solution to the problems above

---

Again, the idea behind "building to think" is to learn fast, fail fast, and therefore learn and fail cheaply.

---

o Define the data and configuration needed for each Use Case or scenario

o Configure and develop the Use Cases or scenarios

o **Demonstrate** the Use Cases or scenarios to the team

o **Iterate** and elaborate on these Use Cases or scenarios based on the feedback and other lessons learned

o **Demonstrate** the Use Case or scenario to the user community identified earlier, and potentially iterate again

Discovery intentionally pushes out the formal start of Execution so we can execute smarter. Once Discovery is complete, we would push our learnings back into the Statement of Work, the Program and Project Management Plans, our schedule, and Lessons Learned register.

Because all of these updates are necessarily time-consuming, it is important to perform and learn from Discovery as soon as it is possible and makes sense from a timing perspective.

Execution Processes

The Project Management Institute (2017) describes several core processes related to Program and Project execution. Here we have combined several, but they essentially remain the same:

- Direct and Manage the Work
- Perform Knowledge Management
- Manage Quality
- Continue Acquiring and Managing Resources
- Manage and Develop Teams
- Manage Communications
- Respond to and Manage Risks
- Perform Procurement Activities
- Manage Stakeholder Engagement

Let us next look at each of these processes through the lens of applied Design Thinking.

Directing and Managing the Work

The work and value of a Program or Project comes as a result of helping our teams work together to complete their scheduled tasks. The end results of these tasks are called Work Products or Deliverables; it is in the form of deliverables that Program or Project value and benefits are realized.

As we review our list of deliverables, we should confirm that they correlate to the complexity of the project. A three-month Project should not have 50 deliverables, for example, nor should a three-year Program have only five.

We need to manage and direct our teams to ensure they make progress on their deliverables. This means verifying that the work gets done as scheduled, spot checking that work, and confirming it meets requirements, conforms to project and quality standards, and more.

Standards for work products and deliverables are established as part of the project planning process (refer back to Chapter 3 starting on p. 50).

Standards include templates, tools, review process, approval process, and ownership of the work product or deliverable. With regard to execution and deliverables, keep the following factors in mind.

- Do we **Understand Broadly** our deliverables users' macro-environment and **Empathize** their needs, including *how* they will use these deliverables and other outcomes?

- Is a **Persona Analysis** called for? For example, if a document deliverable is intended for a group of *business* users, is it safe to exclude technical or other seemingly non-relevant information from that document? Who makes these decisions?

- What **Collaboration** tools and approaches will be used to develop deliverables and get the work done? Is there consensus around the tools and approaches?

- Is the deliverable a one-use or enduring artifact or will it become a living artifact or document updated regularly throughout the Program or Project (and after)?

- In the case of living artifacts or documents, how shall we align its development and future updates to our **Time Horizons**?

- Are we following the **Principle of "No Surprises"** regarding user interfaces, artifacts, and deliverables? Are our designs intuitive or do they confound and confuse? Are we using **Standardized Templates** for consistency and consumability?

- Should we execute an early peer-review before any users see and help us iterate on the deliverable? Or would building a peer review cycle into the schedule just slow us down?

- As we work through our deliverables and other outcomes, how often are we re-visiting our **Customer Journey Maps**? Are we still aligned? Does our work still align with customer touchpoints?

- What is our cadence for performing iteration or solution **Demonstrations**, showcasing **Prototypes**, and in other ways instrumenting and executing our **Feedback Loops**?

- Are we spending too much valuable time on **Demonstrations**? Should we divert that time back to working on the **Prototype** or actual solution iterations?

- Who will review and approve the deliverables and other artifacts?

- What is the cadence for updating the **Lessons Learned** register? Does the broader team have sufficient access to make these updates themselves? Do we have a bottleneck in this regard?

- Which of **Cobb's Paradox** implications (see Figure 10.2 below) do we still need to consider during execution? Are changes affecting executive or stakeholder support, requirements clarity, or our ability to set realistic expectations? Are the right users involved at the right times?

Managing work product completion is an important part of tracking the overall progress of the project. Ensure our development, delivery, review, and other processes and tools can **Scale for Effectiveness**.

SUCCESS CRITERIA	MAX POINTS
1. User Involvement	19
2. Executive Management Support	16
3. Clear Statement of Requirements	15
4. Proper Planning	11
5. Realistic Expectations	10
6. Smaller Project Milestones	9
7. Competent Staff	8
8. Ownership	6
9. Clear Vision & Objectives	3
10. Hard-Working, Focused Staff	3
TOTAL	100

Figure 10.2 Note the relative weight of various Success Criteria in Cobb's matrix.

Performing Knowledge Management

As we progress on our Program or Project, it is important to use the knowledge our broader organization and our local teams already possess. A Knowledge Repository should be in place before execution commences. And for real-time knowledge sharing, consider how we might integrate and connect our people and teams both formally and informally (akin to a really broad **Buddy System**).

Finally, schedule and plan for capturing future **Lessons Learned.** Set up prescribed cadences and checkpoints to gently remind the team of its importance. As we have said before, if something is not in the schedule then it probably won't get done.

Managing Quality

During execution, we must make our Quality Management Plan "real" by delivering in a way that conforms to our standards. Deliverables need to be associated with quality-related requirements or **Guiding Principles**, measurable quality metrics, and quality checklists. Our project schedule also needs to reflect point-in-time quality audits or checkpoints.

Acquiring and Managing Resources

While resource management activities do indeed occur throughout the execution of a Program or Project, many resources are acquired well before execution starts. For our purposes, we want to make sure our people and teams are onboarded and mobilized as discussed in Chapter 9, and incorporate **Time Pacing** and **Scaling for Effectiveness** as applicable.

Managing and Developing the Teams

Our people and teams are our most important resources, and those resources need to be developed and improved over time. In our experience, it is the interpersonal skills and cultural "nimbleness" that need the most attention, especially as teams grow and shrink and change over time. Pay special attention to changes in culture as described in Chapter 6, shaping it and drawing on it to the benefit of the Program or Project.

In addition, pay particular attention to attrition! Apply the **Five Why's** to understand attrition and to make any called-for changes. Finally, continue to develop the team's **Collaboration** capabilities, self-management skills, bias self-awareness, and how each person deals with conflicts and issues. Provide regular feedback, and when team personnel changes are necessary, make those changes as swiftly and transparently as possible.

Managing Communications

As we outlined in Chapter 5, communications are the lifeblood of a Program or Project. We need a robust set of **Guiding Principles** to drive our "how," and we need active leadership to reinforce and confirm that the myriad of communications activities are indeed completed day by day, week over week. Focus on collecting, creating, distributing, storing, retrieving, and managing only what is needed, keeping in mind that communications needs will change over time.

Responding to and Managing Risks

During the Initiate phase, we established a risk management plan. Now we need to regularly evaluate risks, respond to those that have been realized, adjust our plans, and plan for new risks and their mitigations.

Divergent Thinking, the Inverse Power Law, previous Program and Project Retrospectives and Lessons Learned, and proactive Premortems are fantastic tools for thinking through and developing responses to potential risks.

While it is common practice to focus on unfavorable risks in our risk management plans, we also need to think through favorable or "good" realized risks. For example, if our offshore staffing costs decrease by 15% in the wake of replacing one staffing partner with another, our realized risk will actually have a positive effect on costs.

Performing Procurement Activities

For large Programs and Projects, procurement and funding and contract management are all fundamental aspects of preparation. Sure, we might find ourselves midway through a Project, for example, needing to procure additional people or other resources, but generally these procurement activities are done well before Execution. As explained earlier, activities such as replacing one staffing partner with another will drive procurement activities during Execution, as will changes in scope that require crashing the schedule to stay on track. In these cases, turn to your **Guiding Principles** for handling in-flight procurements.

We also need to think through how we might use Procurement as a strategy for **Scaling for Effectiveness**, or how we might apply **Modular Thinking and Building** to our procurement or contracting strategy.

Managing Stakeholder Engagement

This final execution process is about "communicating and working with stakeholders to meet their needs and expectations, address issues, and foster appropriate stakeholder involvement" (Project Management Institute, 2017, p. 610). We often say that Sponsors and other stakeholders are not managed; their expectations are. Think about it.

The whole idea of this stakeholder engagement process is to increase stakeholder support while working to understand their perspectives and especially any resistance they might have to Program or Project changes or perceived changes.

> *Experience and research show us that the more complex and uncertain the endeavor, the more important it is to manage stakeholder involvement and engagement (Ben Mahmoud-Jouini, Midler, & Silberzahn, 2016).*

Continue to manage this engagement throughout the Program or Project, and particularly during Execution, again using the **Stakeholder Map** and a cadence of strong and regular communications.

Parallel Component Projects

By definition, Programs always comprise Component Projects. But in large complex Projects we will typically find ourselves managing Component Projects, too. We might call them parallel workstreams or initiatives, but these work efforts are large enough and complex enough to warrant their own management, integration, and execution focus. Examples of parallel Component Projects, workstreams, initiatives, or other significant bodies of work may include:

- Offshore development work to build software or solution components that will eventually find their way into the overall Program or Project's solution.

- Testing, where the effort is so complex that it is split into specific types of testing (such as unit testing, end to end process testing, integration testing, performance testing, and user acceptance testing), often executed by a dedicated test team.

- Legacy data transformation, especially when there are multiple existing systems and therefore multiple types and forms of data that might need to be extracted, transformed or cleaned, and loaded into a new system.

- System integration, especially when our requirements tell us that multiple existing systems will need to technically connect and conceptually work with our new solution.

- Solution training and Solution deployments or roll-outs, which for large endeavors could include enough tasks, dependencies, people, and processes to warrant their own Component Projects.

Such work needs to be managed from an Integration perspective, too (outlined in Chapter 3, *Program and Project Management Basics*). The important takeaway here is that these parallel Component Projects often need their own Project leadership. Such leadership would be provided by a dedicated project coordinator or Project Manager reporting to the broader Project Manager or even the Program Manager.

Efficacy and Effectiveness

As we touched on in Chapter 9, Mobilization for Effectiveness, successfully executing a Program or Project requires efficacy and effectiveness. Working hard is not enough; to execute successfully is to achieve outcomes by working through ambiguity, making decisions, and making progress. Every Program and Project faces challenges that the team will need to work through:

- Are decisions being made, or are they being ignored or pushed into the future?

- Are issues being resolved in a timely manner? Are we learning from these issues?

- Are we realizing risks we simply had not foreseen? What is our track record of recovering from such realized risks, and why did we miss them in the first place?

- Do we have effective communication channels (both internally within the teams and externally with our Sponsor, stakeholders, and our various users)?

- Are processes in place that define good Program and Project management practices? Are we following them?

- To what extent are our leaders, stakeholders, and Program or Project Sponsor effective and supportive?

These are important questions to review and assess over time, as they affect efficacy or the ability to get hard things done. Improved processes and mitigations may be needed to facilitate effective (and faster) decision making and communications throughout the lifecycle, too.

Poor efficacy ultimately robs an organization of the ability to transform itself.

Executing to Think

In the same way that we "build to think," we need to improve our understanding as we work by "executing to think" and "refining to think." Doing so allows us to course-correct more quickly while doing the kinds of things that help us make progress. Otherwise we could find ourselves in the grip of *paralysis analysis* where we think too much for too long and lose precious time (and create no value) in the process.

As we "execute to think," we should consider the following:

- What is the minimal viable product (MVP) necessary to obtain benefits of the solution?

- Can we achieve an MVP through an iteration or two, or will it take more cycles?

- Can we realistically push out our Time-to-Value, or are there other factors we need to consider (such as the need to retire an existing solution)?

- What are the trade-offs between delivering an MVP and waiting to deliver a full-featured solution? Can my users execute a part of their job in the new solution and a part in the current solution? Or would this be too confusing or too expensive to orchestrate?

As we move through the Execute Phase, we need to constantly remain aware of the tension between the need to iterate on our work and the need to stop iterating and start delivering something of value.

In our Design Thinking view, making progress is more important than achieving perfection. Do we understand what is **Good Enough** to be deployed? Has our user community corroborated our understanding and signed off on our notion of achieving a "good enough" quality bar in a short time horizon and achieving the fuller solution over a longer time horizon? These are important questions upon which to align early.

Guiding Principles for Executing and Realizing Value

Consider the following guiding principles for applying Design Thinking to Program and Project execution and value realization.

- Think strategically and broadly like a Program or Project, not tactically like a collection of Component Projects, initiatives, workstreams, or teams.

- Execute to Think; get started and iterate!

- Delivery is king and deadlines are golden; progress is more important than perfection.

- Know when to stop iterating and put a stake in the ground; improve until good enough, but not beyond.

- Know when to stop optimizing and start repeatably executing; we eventually need to quit tweaking our processes in favor of executing repeatably and consistently.

- If you cannot articulate a problem, do not try to solve it; return to the people affected by the problem. Hear their **Stories**. Enlist others' help and work to improve your broad understanding, your knowledge, and your empathy of those affected.

- Regular instrumented feedback is essential; poor connections back to our users drive knee-jerk changes in both tactical execution and even strategic direction.

- Leaders need to remove blockers to open the door to progress; give leaders a chance to use their blockade-removing skills.

- Give people and teams the chance to do their job, but monitor their understanding, collaboration, and progress.

- Teams might own deliverables, but individuals get them done.

- Hang on to simplicity until it's unable to compete with reality.

- Again, few things enduring or worthwhile are executed solo; validate that team collaboration and user feedback cycles are in place and effective.

- Do not allow the urgent to *constantly* distract you from the important.

- Poor efficacy robs an organization of the ability to get the hard things done necessary to transform itself long-term; be on the lookout for those Efficacy Bandits.

Summary

This chapter walked us through the Execute Phase as we applied Design Thinking to our Programs and Projects. We looked at the value and process of executing Discovery pre-execution, and then explored the various processes underpinning execution. Along the way, we considered a myriad of techniques to help speed us along, and we outlined the work of executing parallel Component Projects, executing to think, and keeping an eye on our overall progress and efficacy.

All of the Design Thinking techniques explored here and elsewhere are outlined in Appendix B, *Design Thinking Techniques*, starting on p. 196.

Case Study

The Harmony Program is on the verge of starting execution of its global business transformation Program and three Projects (Customer Connections Management or CMM, Shipping for Velocity or S4V, and Analytics for Business or A4B). The PMO and Program Director are worried and have a number of questions for you.

Chapter 10 Questions

1. What are the nine core execution processes as described here in Chapter 10?

2. Why will the Harmony Program benefit from a Discovery exercise prior to actually starting Execution?

3. Which Design Thinking techniques should we consider as we go about managing risks and executing our risk responses?

4. Beyond our three formal Component Projects (CMM, S4V, and A4B), what other bodies of work might warrant similar attention and management?

5. What is the connection between efficacy or effectiveness and our ability to complete this Program?

See Appendix A starting on p. 187 for Case Study answers.

Chapter 11

Governing, Controlling, and Monitoring

- o *Delivering what was Promised*
- o *Governance Bodies*
- o *Tools for Governing, Controlling, and Monitoring*
- o *Key Governance and Controlling Processes*
- o *Key Monitoring Processes*
- o *Monitoring our Culture and Health*
- o *Monitoring Benefits Realization*
- o *Guiding Principles for Governing, Controlling, and Monitoring*
- o *Chapter Summary and Case Study*

Governance is about confirming that what has been promised is actually being delivered throughout the Program or Project, and it helps ensure that the overall work remains on plan (see Figure 11.1).

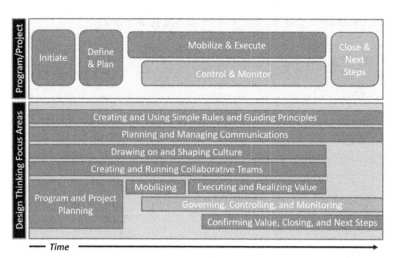

Figure 11.1 Governing, Controlling, and Monitoring commence before execution.

In Chapter 11, we review the Project Management Institute's (2017) Monitoring and Controlling process group to confirm progress, track variances, and make course corrections. We expand on this guidance to also include what it means to drive clarity, govern benefits realization, and monitor the health of our people and teams.

Delivering what was Promised

In our context, governance is the act of overseeing a Program or Project across its lifecycle. This oversight starts before Execution, and in reality governance processes may be put in place as early as the Initiate phase.

We are fond of joking that governance is akin to babysitting and providing adult supervision, but it is truly much more. Governance is about discipline and accountability and responsibility, all of which are driven through an intentional governance model. In turn, the model must reflect purpose-built communications and controls on behalf of a Program's or Project's Sponsor and other stakeholders (Alie, 2015).

Only through consistently executed governance processes can a Program or Project Manager deliver promised benefits, value, and other outcomes.

To be clear, the PMO is responsible for governance operations most broadly, working with the Steering Committee to make decisions and address issues. But on one end of the governance spectrum, the Sponsor plays the key role in setting strategic direction, while on the other end of the spectrum the Program or Project Manager is accountable for managing and executing governance processes.

Governance Bodies

As the core governance body, the Program or Project Management Office controls and monitors task progress and completion. The PMO sets the standard and tone for how things get done. The PMO is therefore the primary Governance Body; all other bodies need to operate "through" and defer to the PMO's governance standards and processes.

As we see in Figure 11.2 and the list below, at least three additional governance bodies play important roles working alongside the PMO helping to govern aspects of a Program or Project:

- The **Executive Steering Committee** serves as the PMO's governance "supervisory board," helping to ensure that Program and Project issues are addressed, decisions are timely, schedule timelines are preserved, and outside dependencies are understood. In large organizations, this executive board might comprise a Senior Executive Steering Committee and a more tactical or "operational" *Working Steering Committee*.

- The **Architecture Review Board** provides governance around the Program's or Project's solution and solutioning activities (including governance related to ideating, prototyping and building, testing, and iterating on the solution). Here we are talking about the real solution being deployed as part of a business or operational transformation.

- The **Change Control Board (CCB)** reviews, approves (or delays or denies), and manages the inevitable Program/Project-related Scope of Work changes.

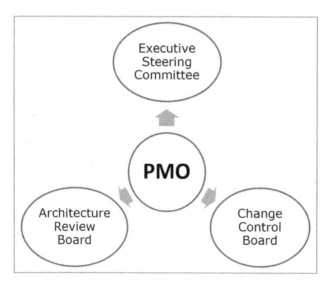

Figure 11.2 The four key Governance Bodies and primary governing role of the PMO.

Other special-purpose governance bodies may be established as well. For large packaged software Programs and Projects, for example, a Fit/Gap Review Board considers customization-vs-configuration implications and ensures that departures from standards benefit from additional governance and visibility.

Mock-Ups, **Rapid Prototyping**, and limited **Proofs of Concept** or **Pilots** play roles in helping the decision-making process around these potential departures from the Program's or Project's standards. These Design Thinking techniques are pursued in the context of the **Customer Journey Map** (while considering user experience and Program/Project financials and risks). The team might re-visit **Problem Definition** as well, simply to confirm that the right problem is truly solved by a proposed method for addressing a Gap.

For smaller or less complex Programs and Projects, the Architecture Review Board may perform the role of the Fit/Gap Review Board. The ARB would actually pick up any other technical or solution-related responsibilities otherwise farmed out to special-purpose governance bodies. In addition, the ARB considers architectural implications such as:

- Assessing and instituting new architectural **Patterns**
- Helping teams think through solutioning strategies and either pursue or avoid **Adjacent Spaces**
- Making architectural strategy decisions related to **Time Horizons** or the business impact of **Time Pacing** realities
- Executing **CARMA Analyses** when options need to be quantified and compared across cost as well as risk dimensions
- Providing guidance and risk opinions reflecting the organization's appetite for **Crowd Sourcing**-based solutioning
- Thinking through the technical viability and options to explore **Mutating on More than one Gene**

Finally, the Change Control Board or CCB also develops and adheres to a stringent set of change control processes to manage Program and Project changes. The CCB creates a standard Change Control template (an example of a **Standardized Template**, explained on p. 206) for managing and documenting proposed changes, too. Typical contents of this Change Control template include:

- A name and a control number for the proposed change
- The date of the change request

- The requestor's name

- A description of the existing (currently scoped) solution

- A description of the proposed change to the solution

- The business justification for the proposed change

- The technical or other justification for the proposed change

- How the proposed change is expected to affect the current implementation approach and overall timing

- The impact of the proposed change on the current project schedule (including how long it will take to plan for the change, prototype and build the change, test the change, and deploy it)

- The expected cost of the proposed change

Meetings and other status mechanisms are fundamental governance tools. Let us now look at other these and other tools and methods used for governing, controlling, and monitoring.

Tools for Governing, Controlling, and Monitoring

Communications underpins governance. The key is to identify and use the right kinds of communications tools for the right audiences. In our experience, it is critical to establish a strong cadence of Board and Committee meetings:

- As a first step, identify and confirm membership for each of the Boards, Committees, and other such governance-related teams.

- Executive Steering Committees should meet at least monthly (though senior executive boards might meet every six to eight weeks once the work is well underway, while their operational counterparts continue to meet monthly).

- The Architecture Review Board should meet weekly initially, and potentially every two weeks once the work is well underway.

- The Change Control Board must meet at least weekly if not more frequently, depending on the volume and nature of proposed scope changes.

- If a Fit/Gap Review Board has been established, it benefits most from an ad hoc schedule predicated on the timely review of gaps as those gaps are identified. Set up a weekly cadence for starters, and change the frequency as needed.

Meetings are effective tools, but people and teams also need to be proactively alerted to current state; trends, issues and other realized risks; current tasks or work-in-progress; late work and upcoming work; and so on. This is where custom-built workstream, swim-lane, and other Program and Project dashboards and reports are essential.

For maximum visibility and transparency, work with the team to design and deploy its individual team member dashboards, team-specific dashboards, and workstream-specific dashboards.

Use tools such as Visual Studio Team Services or its successor Azure DevOps, and GitHub, and other. The idea is to practice the **Principle of "No Surprises"** broadly, from dashboard usability to visibility into status, needs, and other information.

Beyond regular meeting cadences and purpose-built team-specific and other dashboards, consider the following:

- Push regular status reports to specific user communities weekly.

- Enable publish/subscribe capabilities to consume other types of reports that users might be interested in or need-to-know.

- Alert users when new documents are posted to a collaboration site or updates are made to key documents (such as the **Lessons Learned** register).

- Make key calendar events visible, including scheduled **Prototyping** efforts, the start of new iterations, solution **Demonstrations**, and **Ideation** and **Brainstorming** sessions.

- Use **Collaboration** tools such as Microsoft Teams and Slack to stand up Program/Project-specific collaboration and file sharing spaces, enable instant messaging and video/voice calling, provide Knowledge Management capabilities, persist team discussions, and track and convert discussions into action items.

Key Governance and Controlling Processes

With a sense of the kinds of tools available, let us turn our attention to the governing and controlling processes framed as knowledge areas by the Project Management Institute (2017). The processes below give you a sense of the breadth of governance and control activities.

- Scope validation and scope control. Ensure you are delivering precisely what has been agreed to be delivered. Forward proposed changes to the Change Control Board for broad visibility and consideration.

- Schedule and cost control. Ensure you are managing and controlling the schedule and costs on at least a weekly cadence. Variations in schedule will also reveal variances elsewhere (employ the **Five Why's** to understand the full picture and what may be changing underfoot); pay attention to the schedule.

- Quality control. Enlist a quality-focused team member or outside auditor to review Program and Project outputs, artifacts, and other deliverables. The quality control process will help spot deviations, remedy those deviations, and it should conclude by pointing us back to updating the **Lessons Learned** register.

- Resource control. Manage and control resource utilization against expected utilization; investigate deltas and take corrective action. In cases where people (our key resources) seem to be taking too long to complete their tasks, consider whether there is adequate **Problem Definition** and clarity. Has the work fundamentally changed? Would their tasks benefit from better **Prototyping**, better **Standardized Templates**, improved **Story Boarding, Broader Understanding**, or something similar? Is it time to engage in a markedly different kind of approach (such as **Reverse-Brainstorming**, the **Speed Boat and Anchors** exercise, or **Divergent Thinking**)? Are the right resources with the right skills in the right roles, or are we confusing misplaced team member compassion with empathy?

- Overall performance. Compare actual Program or Project performance to planned performance (including schedule, deliverables, activities, resource utilization, costs, and more) and assess the deltas. If specific teams tend to fall short, help them revisit their **Simple Rules, Guiding Principles**, issues faced, and track record of efficacy and effectiveness. Ensure they understand the work and environment, have the tools they need, are staffed with the right people possessing the right skills, and are practicing the right kinds of Design Thinking techniques to help them work though questions and accelerate delivery.

It is important to perform these processes systematically and routinely. Establish a cadence of governance (in the same way we establish meeting cadences), and instrument alerts to proactively identify variances, trends, and outright issues.

The failure to achieve Program and Project goals is usually the result of one or more of these processes spiraling out of control. Successful Programs and Projects therefore devote a good amount of energy to these areas. As **Cobb's Paradox** tells us, we all know that these things are important, yet we still tend to underestimate that importance. Establish and maintain strong diligence in these areas early on:

- Project scope is preserved (plus or minus approved changes)

- Project budgets and costs are on plan

- Planned work product and deliverables quality is directionally aligned or achieved

- Necessary testing and other validations are indeed executed

- Overall variances from plan are captured, synthesized, and shared with the appropriate team members and project stakeholders

The next set of activities focus on monitoring rather than governing and controlling.

Key Monitoring Processes

In terms of monitoring, there are several key processes to keep an eye on. The goal is to help ensure good project execution by monitoring data confirming that the overall work, scope, costs, schedule, quality, and so on remain on plan.

The Project Management Institute (2017) calls out four specific knowledge areas or processes that require careful monitoring: communications, risks, stakeholder engagement, and the overall work (set of tasks outlined in a Project Plan/WBS). Each of these is outlined next with an eye towards applying Design Thinking to monitor these processes better or more easily.

Monitoring Communications

As we have said before, the heart of an effective Program or Project often rests in good communication and **Collaboration** processes. However, it is critical that the team and its people actually *use* the communications tools and practices that the team has agreed to use. For example:

- If the team or leaders have agreed to use a collaboration site or tool, verify its consistent use and work to understand why the tool in some cases or by some users is *not* being adopted.

- If the team has agreed that links to documents rather than email attachments will be shared through email and collaboration tools, monitor compliance and gently nudge violators back on track.

- If the team is supposed to use specific distribution lists to help ensure people are not left out of important communiques, verify they are being used.

Spot check whether the right people are getting the right information at the right time; simply ask them if they have what they need when they need it.

Look back at Chapter 5 on Communications for other ideas and practices to help bolster your communications monitoring strategy.

Monitoring Risks and Issues

Unlike the risk reviews and time invested executing our responses to risks, we also need to regularly think ahead about potential and unrealized risks, ready to act should those risks materialize into issues.

Identifying and managing project risks and issues is important work, but it can be simplified. In fact, issue management is a very basic process when faced with 15 issues. But the work and the remediation can become much more complex in environments where we are managing 200 potential risks and another 200 actual issues. Staff the PMO's risk and issues team with the appropriate headcount, and then have the team select a risks and issues tool capable of managing the workload. Features of a good risks and issues management tool include:

- The capability to fully describe issues and possible solutions

- The ability to track acceptance criteria to acknowledge when and why issues are closed

- The ability to track the Root Cause Analysis (RCA) process

- The ability to support insights that come out of early **Mind Mapping** and other **Ideation** exercises, **Premortems**, **Divergent Thinking**, and similar techniques

- The ability to model costs and other dimensions or implications alongside risk (or at minimum dump its data into Microsoft Excel to perform a **CARMA Analysis**)

- Strong mechanisms for reporting risks, risk mitigations, open and closed issues, statistics reflecting the movement of risks when they become issues, and other details

Monitoring Stakeholder Engagement

Different than managing stakeholder expectations discussed in Chapter 10, this process is actually related to monitoring how *well* stakeholders stay connected through their various relationships, board and committee participation, and overall visibility. We need to help key stakeholders and the Program or Project Sponsor stay visible and in the center of things by working with their schedules and regularly sharing their thoughts and decisions.

Systematically update the **Stakeholder Map** and register, and assess each stakeholder's participation, attitude, trends (such as no-shows at meetings, or having a delegate show up more often than not). It is better to reschedule Executive Steering Committee meetings, for example, than to cancel them outright or try to execute important decision-making through email.

> *...and remember, Stakeholders and Sponsors need to be seen and heard to be most effective.*

Monitoring the Work

Monitoring that the work is getting done, and done right, is important throughout a Program or Project. Completion of a Project's work products or deliverables, for example, is a simple yet effective measure of work progress. Consider how the **Rule of Threes** plays out (and how this Rule might affect timing and resourcing). Find early opportunities to set and reinforce reasonable expectations while pushing for **Good Enough** outcomes and deliverables; your goal is to meet the quality bar established for the Program or Project, not wildly exceed it.

Deliverables must also be monitored to ensure they live up to agreed-upon quality standards, meet requirements, conform to standards, and therefore meet stakeholder expectations.

As we outlined previously, it is also perfectly natural for scope changes to surface as we execute. Approved changes need to be managed and incorporated into the overall schedule.

Monitoring Team Culture and Health

While not specifically called out by the Project Management Institute as a separate process, the notion of monitoring organizational or team culture and health goes hand-in-hand with managing the work. After all, culture is a resource that needs to be monitored just like any other resource.

Revisit Chapter 6 and consider the following monitoring focus areas:

- Monitor how we are drawing on the organization's and each team's current culture.

- Monitor how we are shaping our culture to redefine over time what it means to be an effective team and supportive organization.

- Monitor to what extent differences are intentionally leveraged for good or take a back seat to achieving the Program's or Project's goals and objectives.

- Confirm that the practice of assigning a person to a particular assignment has nothing to do with differences but rather with capabilities, maturity, and attitude.

- Confirm in cases where someone has infringed upon another's rights or created a less than safe work environment that our leaders took swift steps to remedy the problem while working to understand and change the underlying attitudes or behaviors.

Finally, consider whether a follow-up **Culture Assessment** is in order. As our people and teams develop and are shaped over time, we might want to run a checkpoint against our baseline Culture Assessment. In this way, we can better understand how well our organization and teams have matured, and we can target remaining gaps more precisely.

Monitoring Benefits Realization

Well before a Program or Project is ever closed, we also need to monitor how well and to what extent its expected benefits are being realized and new capabilities being consumed. This monitoring activity should start when Program or Project execution begins if not earlier; instrumentation takes time and the risks of failing to achieve expected benefits make this time and effort worthwhile.

Thus, as soon as we start executing, we need to establish the monitoring and controls necessary to monitor benefits realization. Our monitoring system needs to consider how to answer questions such as:

- Do we have the complete set of expected benefits instrumented to provide the datapoints necessary for monitoring? Can we monitor more than the near-term expected benefits?

- Are we on target to achieve our next set of benefits-related milestones and other checkpoints? How can we be sure?

- Are we missing any key benefits realization or solution adoption datapoints or metrics?

- Where are we at risk of not realizing our expected benefits?

- Have new benefits actually been realized through the adoption of the new solution's capabilities? Are these capabilities being used in the manner expected? By how large a community?

- Are financials, resource plans, schedules, quality, and so on in line with the expected benefits? To what extent do our variances differ from expected? Are we paying too much for these benefits?

Again, a Program or Project should only be closed once stakeholders agree that its expected benefits have been realized. Visibility of metrics and other datapoints related to Program and Project benefits—and the adoption of new capabilities—are key to confirming that realization.

Guiding Principles for Governing, Controlling, and Monitoring

Consider the following Guiding Principles related to governing, controlling, and monitoring:

- Employ lightweight governance until a heavier hand is needed.

- Work through the unknowns but always communicate in facts.

- Iterate on and improve governance, controlling, and monitoring processes until they are good enough, and then simply govern, control, and monitor in repeatable and predictable ways.

- Maintain an action-oriented governance mindset.

- Use governance, controlling, and monitoring processes to help the team stick to their roles; identify over-functioning and remedy those imbalances swiftly.

- Employ the right governance tools and processes for the right users.

- Use governance practices and monitoring processes to support quick decision-making, recognizing that quick decisions grounded in data are key time-to-value enablers.

- Unresolved questions and decisions become issues with broad consequences; govern and control to avoid those consequences.

- A track record of quick yet informed decision-making trumps no decisions and covers over the occasional bad decision.

- Leaders need to govern as if they will own the outcome; they do.

- Culture is a resource that needs to be monitored just like any other resource.

- Controlling and monitoring without a baseline is much less valuable (some would say useless) than comparing current performance against a baseline; think through and collect the relevant datapoints and metrics for monitoring.

Summary

In Chapter 11, we extended the work of Execution outlined in Chapter 10 to include what it means to apply Design Thinking to Governing, Controlling, and Monitoring processes. We discussed how governance is tied to delivering what we have promised (through a Program's or Project's outcomes and benefits), and we outlined several governance bodies and committees. Then we turned our attention to the key governing, controlling, and monitoring processes. We closed the chapter with a discussion on the need to monitor organizational culture, health, and benefits realization including early instrumentation, and we concluded as usual with a set of chapter-specific guiding principles.

All of the Design Thinking techniques explored here and elsewhere are outlined in Appendix B, *Design Thinking Techniques*, starting on p. 196.

Case Study

As the Harmony Program works through execution, several of the PMO's team members have expressed concern around a lack of strong governance, control, and monitoring. The Program seems to be moving along, but it is unclear whether or not the three Component Projects (CMM, S4V, and A4B) are making real progress. Visibility and accountability seem to be missing. The Program Director has come to you for advice.

Chapter 11 Questions

1. What governing, controlling, and monitoring tools should we consider beyond establishing meeting cadences and setting up team-specific and other dashboards?

2. What are the five governing and controlling processes outlined in this chapter?

3. What are the four key monitoring processes outlined here?

4. The Program Director is concerned about the CMM Component Project's team culture. What is your perspective regarding monitoring culture, and what five areas or factors should be monitored?

See Appendix A starting on p. 187 for Case Study answers.

Chapter 12

Confirming Value, Closing, and Next Steps

- *Confirming Value and Benefits Realization*
- *Concluding a Program or Project*
- *Thinking through Next Steps*
- *Guiding Principles for Closing Programs and Projects*
- *Chapter Summary and Case Study*

Properly closing a Program or Project means more than just delivering a solution and gaining signoff from the Sponsor that the work has been completed. On the contrary, there are specific processes and tasks to be executed prior to closing. The solution's value and benefits need to be confirmed, specific people need to confirm that value, other people need to be transitioned out, still others may need to be transitioned in, paperwork needs to be completed, and agreements closed or terminated. In this final chapter, we look at applying Design Thinking to Closing and Next Steps.

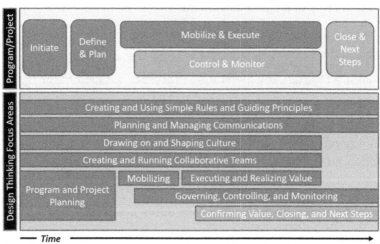

Figure 12.1 Closing includes confirming Value and thinking through next steps.

Confirming Value and Benefits Realization

As we outlined in Chapter 11, actually monitoring Benefits Realization is important throughout a Program or Project (rather than exclusively at the end). In the same way, we need to confirm prior to Closing that the intended value and benefits have indeed been fully delivered. How? By performing the following:

- Confirm with the Sponsor that the Program or Project Charter's strategy and benefits have been achieved (taking approved changes into account).

- Validate with users that the benefits they expected are being provided by the deployed solution (adoption is the key after all; solutions must be adopted/used to actually prove useful).

- Validate with stakeholders and users that all deliverables and other work products have indeed been delivered, and that living documents or artifacts have undergone their final updates prior to Program or Project closure.

- Working with the PMO and relevant stakeholders, confirm that the Benefits Management Plan includes a Benefits Maximization plan to ensure that the solution's benefits and other capabilities are expanded, extended, or otherwise maximized over time.

- Similarly, confirm that the Benefits Management Plan also includes a Benefits Sustainment plan to ensure that the solution's benefits continue to be monitored and curated long after the Program or Project is closed.

Note that each task above includes both a unique "What" and an important "Who."

Confirming value and Benefits Realization means hearing directly from our Sponsors, stakeholders, and particularly our users that they received or are receiving the benefits they expected to receive.

Concluding a Program or Project

Concluding a Program or Project involves executing a set of closing processes that formally wind down and ultimately terminate or "close" all of its activities. Keep in mind that a successful solution deployment or "go-live" does not close a Program or Project… nor does completing the remaining tasks outlined in a work breakdown structure….or consuming all of its budget… or losing the Executive Sponsor. Closing is a formal process, and those closing-related processes and tasks include the following (refer to Appendix B, *Design Thinking Techniques*, starting on p. 196 for additional details related to the **bold** items here):

- Capture final **Lessons Learned**. Prior to closing, run a session to capture any final learnings and record those learnings in the Lessons Learned register (which should have been regularly updated throughout the Program or Project).

- Archive Knowledge. Ensure all Program and Project learnings and knowledge maintained in the Knowledge Management system are archived for future reference and for use by others.

- Complete and confirm completion of all Planned Work. Though it probably goes without saying, ensure that any remaining tasks and **Deliverables** are completed and published or shared as planned.

- Perform remaining Administrative Tasks. Record any final acceptance of the Program's or Project's work products and deliverables, perform final financial and budget updates and reconciliation, and transition Program or Project operations and open issues to the responsible parties who will own those operations and issues post-closing.

- Obtain Formal Signoff. Programs and Projects are not officially closed until their Sponsors and key stakeholders agree that what was set to be accomplished through the Project Charter has indeed been accomplished (plus or minus any approved changes). Such sign-off or formal acceptance of the solution needs to be captured in writing.

- Close Contracts. Once sign-off or formal acceptance is received, the Program or Project can be closed from a legal perspective. In this way, contracts can be concluded or terminated, third party subcontractors and other providers can be properly released, billing and expenses can be processed, purchase orders can be properly closed, and more.

- Release Resources. With everything else in order, the Program's or Project's staff and other resources may finally be released (though as we will explore later in this chapter, we may prefer to transition them to a planned follow-on endeavor rather than release them outright to pursue other opportunities).

- Complete any Organization-specific processes. It is common for organizations to execute their own set of specific processes when they shut down a Program or Project or conclude a contract. This might include conducting Sponsor, stakeholder, and user satisfaction surveys, performing a **Retrospective**, publishing final stakeholder status reports and other reports, sharing Value/Benefits Realization outcomes, sharing next steps with the organization's leadership team, and executing a **Postmortem**.

With value and benefits confirmed and our Program or Project formally concluded, it is tempting to think we have reached the end. But we really need to fight the urge to just pack up and head home.

The opportunities to build upon our deployed solution, or further leverage our teams and their ability to get hard things done, are too valuable to pass up.

Thinking through Next Steps

Well before a Program or Project is closed, the Sponsor and other stakeholders need to plan for "What's Next." We call this **Next Step Thinking,** and it is an important part of capitalizing on our investments and delivering value beyond *Today*.

- Extend the current Program or Project to **Iterate** on or improve the capabilities of the current solution for its existing user community.

- Extend the current Program or Project to add capabilities or specifically address **Inclusive or Sensitive Design** (usability gaps) of the current solution for a *new* user community.

- Work with the Sponsor to expand the current Program's or Project's **Charter** to pursue **Adjacent Spaces** or **Co-Innovation** opportunities, address **Minimalism** goals, or seek out new value by **Mutating on More than One Gene** or **Regenerating through Combining**.

- Work with current or new Stakeholders to focus on organizational longevity by **Tossing out Traditional Strategies** in favor of Design Thinking-inspired strategies.

- **Re-purpose** the existing Program/Project Team for a similar endeavor elsewhere in the organization. For instance, rather than expanding on the current solution, we might prefer to redeploy a healthy and proven team to complete a similar piece of work for the organization. The team would ramp up and more quickly deliver value than any newly assembled team could.

This final example can be seen in our Case Study for this chapter (p. 185), where we transition the CMM Component Project Team to design and deliver a 4th Component Project for the Harmony Program.

Guiding Principles for Closing and Thinking through Next Steps

Consider the following principles for closing and next steps:

- Not all problems can be solved with the time or resources allotted; become a master at delivering value within the boundaries of the Program or Project.

- The Important is more critical than the Urgent; ensure that the Important is delivered prior to closing.

- Use "Next Step thinking" to deliver value tomorrow that simply cannot be delivered today.

- In the same way that we "met the customer where they are" back in the beginning of the Program or Project, we need to Close by thinking about what the customer either still needs or now needs in light of what was just delivered.

- Capitalize on the intrinsic value of the assembled Team, solution and processes, and efficacy to continue delivering value in some form or fashion well after the current Program or Project is closed.

Summary

In Chapter 12, we reviewed the processes used to conclude our work. We reviewed the importance of confirming a Program's or Project's value and benefits, and concluded with thoughts on how we might continue to build on our newly delivered solution and further leverage our time-tested and effective teams.

All of the Design Thinking techniques explored here and elsewhere are outlined in Appendix B, *Design Thinking Techniques*, starting on p. 196.

Case Study

Two of the Component Projects within the Harmony Program umbrella are in the process of closing. The Program Director has asked you for your thoughts on how to effectively close the CMM Component Project, and is curious about your thoughts on Next Steps in light of a recently approved 4th Component Project.

Chapter 12 Questions

1. In what way might the effective and healthy CMM Component Project team prove useful for the Harmony Program's upcoming 4th Component Project?

2. The S4V Component Project is also closing soon, but that Project's Sponsor is working to extend the Project and potentially expand its Charter. In what ways might the current S4V project team provide value if they're asked to stay with the S4V Project?

3. The CMM Project Manager wants to know more about what it means to "wrap up the final learnings" and preserve the CMM Component Project's knowledge?

4. Which two plans within the Benefits Management Plan need to be in place and confirmed by the PMO and relevant Stakeholders to ensure ongoing value and benefits realization?

5. What are the six activities that the CMM Project Manager needs to ensure occur before the staff can be released to join the 4th Component Project?

See Appendix A starting on p. 187 for Case Study answers.

APPENDICES
& REFERENCES

Appendix A

Case Study Answers

Chapter 1 Answers. Why Design Thinking?

1. Program and Project Management is the "wrapper" around a solution to be delivered; P&PM safeguards, protects, and helps ensure that the actual solution is indeed designed, developed, and deployed. P&PM acts like the protective sheath of a power cord, helping ensure the wire it safeguards (that is, the actual business transformation or solution) delivers its power/value.

2. There are many more than five Perils, including the Staffing Sand Trap, the Capability Chasm or Cliff, the Culture Comet, the Governance Distractions, the Data & Integrations Firestorms, the Funding or Budget Bridges, the Contracts and software/IP licensing Mudslide, the Sponsorship Volcano, the Change Wave, the Efficacy Bandits (and many others).

3. Applying Design Thinking to Program and Project Management processes and methods gives us the freedom and flexibility to tackle unknowns, and to learn and iterate on those learnings when we need to do so—all in the name of moving more quickly.

4. The real value and answer to the question "Why Design Thinking?" lies in the notion of improved Time-to-Value.

5. From a time-frame perspective, Best and Common Practices provide point-in-time advice and guidance. Simple Rules and Guiding Principles, on the other hand, provide longer-term guidance.

Chapter 2 Answers. What is Design Thinking?

1. The five steps or five components of the *Design Thinking Model for Program and Project Management*, in order, are Understand broadly; Empathize with users; Define the problem; Ideate, Prototype, Test, Iterate, and Build the solution (the sum of which is also called Solutioning); and Deploy to users.

2. Though absent in many other Design Thinking models, the fifth step or component was added to the *Design Thinking Model for Program and Project Management* because benefits realization in

the form of solution deployment and user adoption is always our goal. Further, in our world of large-scale Program and Project Management, deployment itself can be incredibly complex or unique, demanding its own round of Design Thinking.

3.   The five-components of the Design Thinking model should inform every aspect or phase of traditional Program and Project Management, from Initiate to Define and Plan, to Mobilize and Execute, to Control and Monitor, to Close and Next Steps.

4.   The Design Thinking component "Understand Broadly" means first exploring an organization's industry, environment, in-process or pending economic or regulatory changes, and more. Then it is necessary to find out more about the all-up organization itself. Finally, we need to learn more about the specific Business Units with which we will be working/engaging.

5.   The notion of "Building to Think" values doing over lots and lots of planning and thinking and more planning. The idea is that we will learn more quickly about a user's needs if we begin actually prototyping and getting feedback on a potential solution as quickly as possible.

Chapter 3 Answers. Program and Project Management Basics

1.   Programs are strategic in nature, delivering value through a complex collection of Component Projects and potentially other initiatives and dependencies. Projects on the other hand are execution-focused and therefore more tactical in nature.

2.   Program Management is concerned with five strategic "management" processes including Strategy Management, Benefits Management, Stakeholder Engagement Management, Program Life Cycle Management, and Program Governance.

3.   The five phases of Program and Project Management based on the Project Management Institute's perspective and influenced by Design Thinking include Initiate, Define and Plan, Mobilize and Execute, Control and Monitor, and Close and Next Steps.

4.   While controlling and monitoring a Program or Project, it is important to escalate significant and unresolvable issues quickly to the appropriate governance body. Such escalation is both expected and appropriate. Do not be afraid to escalate problems fast and high to executive decision-makers; they expect to be called upon to act as tiebreakers and to make difficult decisions. Use them.

Chapter 4 Answers. Simple Rules and Guiding Principles

1.   Drafting Simple Rules is a team endeavor; the team that is asked to live by a set of rules needs a hand in crafting (and buying in) to those Rules.

2.   Simple Rules describe Who we are, What we do (and don't do), and When we do it (or don't do it). Guiding Principles reflect an organization's core values and add the dimension of How to these Rules.

3.   A Brainstorming session could easily yield 30+ Simple Rules. Before the session concludes, however, the team needs to find and agree on the *themes* that allow for about 10 Rules. Once these Rules are used a while, the team should be able to further whittle them down to the five or six Rules to live by.

4.   Simple Rules are synonymous with a team or organization's vision and goals which can change over time (granted, the lower-level and more focused the team, the less likely such changes will occur). However, Guiding Principles reflect the core values of the team or organization, such as honesty or transparency, and therefore tend to be longer-term and non-negotiable.

Chapter 5 Answers. Communications

1.   Seven areas where we can apply design thinking include Empathy through Listening; Questioning Deeply; Brainstorming the Critical or Enduring; Communicating Visually; Communicating through Stories; Prototyping Methods and Channels; and Empathy through Realized Changes.

2.   Beyond pictures, figures, and graphs, animated content and videos can communicate complex processes repeatably and consistently. So too can "structured text" when words are deemed necessary.

3.   Stories are rarely a good fit for status updates and executive or other stakeholder updates.

4.   In Design Thinking, teams usually spend their time empathizing with users. However, in this case where empathy is derived

through realized changes, we see users empathizing with the team seeking to help the users; the empathy comes as a result of realized changes and seeing real progress (no matter how small that progress might be). Thus, empathy through realized changes flips the user/team source/target relationship and flow of empathy, a marked departure from the usual.

Chapter 6 Answers. Drawing on and Shaping Culture

1. Consider the Culture Onion as a way to view the layers of culture (layers inform and affect one another); consider the Culture Cube when it comes to dimensions of culture.

2. The three dimensions of the Culture Cube are Environment, Work Climate, and Work Style; "missed deadlines" from a cultural sense might tie back best to Work Style, specifically the "Timing" perspective or dynamic.

3. A four-step process or exercise for assessing and shaping culture includes:

    1. Understand and baseline the present culture

    2. Model the future culture

    3. Develop a culture transformation roadmap/plan

    4. Execute, evaluate, and iterate

4. Cultural intelligence is measured by observing or asking questions related to many different areas such as how the team addresses planning, decision making, communications, and collaboration; how the team views time; to what extent the team values caring for self vs caring for others; how the team thinks about and how it works within a hierarchy; how the team thinks about introducing and adopting changes; and how the team views the needs of work against the needs of family, community, society, and other priorities.

Chapter 7 Answers. Creating and Running Collaborative Teams

1. An effective and collaborative team member needs to operate with self-awareness and self-management ("bias awareness"); courageous perspectives shared through respectful person-to-person communications; strong initiative and enduring

motivation; situationally-aware leadership and equally adept follower-ship; and superb conflict management skills and the ability to work with anyone

2.   The story of the circle, the rectangle, and the cylinder illustrates the notion that teams benefit from including team members with different perspectives. Otherwise we can fail to see the whole picture.

3.   Design Thinking tells us to "build to think" to help us avoid thinking and planning so long that most of our learnings occur late in the solutioning process. Action bias, or the notion that it is better to do "something" than nothing, is counterproductive due to a lack of understanding or information supporting the "something" leading to wasted time and effort.

4.   Transparency reinforces both accountability and trust; through visibility and consequences, transparency drives greater accountability which in turns helps teams trust one another to do what they said they were going to do.

Chapter 8 Answers. Program and Project Planning

1.   The Program or Project initiator or Sponsor publishes the Program or Project Charter, which is the key foundational document and serves as the overall "starting point" for everything. The charter documents the high-level project description and boundaries, requirements, risks, stakeholders, summarized milestones, key deliverables, success criteria, preapproved financial resources, and more.

2.   To determine the type of PMO to create, consider employing Brainstorming, performing a Culture Assessment, and applying Modular Thinking to determine the components of and start designing a best-fit PMO.

3.   To create repeatable and consistent plans, artifacts and other documents, start first with a Standardized Template; such templates help us move quickly through the "build" process while helping to ensure we do not miss anything mandatory or foundational.

4. Prior to creating Program and Project Plans and other artifacts, we should employ Empathy Mapping or perform a lightweight Persona Analysis of each Plan's or artifact's user community (each audience or set of readers). Doing so will help us learn our audience and therefore consistently "write" to or create for that audience.

Chapter 9 Answers. Mobilizing for Effectiveness

1. The specific Perils we covered in this chapter include Staffing; Capabilities; Funding, Budgets, and Contracts; Sponsorship; Change Readiness; and Efficacy Blockers.

2. The Onboarding Package should include a high-level synopsis of the Program's Vision; Scope of Work; a high-level Program Roadmap or Schedule of milestones; the list of key Work Products to be created; the Program's Stakeholder Map and pertinent analysis; site logistics (such as security considerations and key contact information); work standards and tools (including access to those tools and basic "How to Use" guidance); a high-level view of the implementation methodology; and the team's communication norms and expectations.

3. Readiness for change should span business change management, Program-specific change control, and technology team IT changes.

4. Efficacy blockers are anything that gets in the way of getting hard things done. Look at an organization's past track record of getting (and not getting) hard things done to understand its blockers. And pay attention to Cobb's Paradox which tells us we need strong Project Managers and standardized project management processes among other factors.

Chapter 10 Answers. Executing and Realizing Value

1. The core execution processes described in this chapter include direct and manage the work; perform knowledge management; manage quality; continue acquiring and managing resources; manage and develop the teams; manage communications; respond to and manage risks; perform procurement activities; and manage stakeholder engagement.

2.   Discovery serves a number of purposes. It confirms our understanding of solution requirements and therefore the Scope of Work; it forces us to revalidate the problems that triggered the Program's or Project's need in the first place; it forces us to revisit the solution we intend to design, development, and deploy to solve those problems; it helps us get more of the team on the same page (the later Discovery is done, presumably the more hiring we have completed); and Discovery serves as a "soft" start to executing as we work through our collaboration, knowledge management, communication, and other processes prior to commencing formal execution.

3.   To help manage risks and execute our risk responses, consider four Design Thinking techniques: Divergent Thinking, the Inverse Power Law, leveraging previous Program and Project Lessons Learned, and executing Premortems.

4.   Beyond Program Harmony's three formal Component Projects, the PMO might need to manage several other large bodies of work as Component Projects including the work of Offshore Development, Testing, Legacy Data transformation, System Integration, and end user Solution Training and Solution Roll-out.

5.   Many factors will naturally affect Program efficacy or the ability to get hard things done. Poor efficacy robs an organization of the ability to transform itself, making it important to track how well we make decisions, address issues, work through realized risks, communicate, and so on.

Chapter 11 Answers. Governing, Controlling, and Monitoring

1.   Beyond meetings and dashboards, push regular status reports out broadly to specific user communities each week; enable publish/subscribe capabilities to consume other types of reports that users might want or need; alert users when new documents or artifacts are posted to a collaboration site or updates are made to those documents or artifacts; make key calendar events visible, and use collaboration tools such as Microsoft Teams and Slack.

2.   The five governing and controlling processes outlined in this chapter include scope validation and scope control; schedule and

cost control; quality control; resource control; and overall performance.

3. The four key monitoring processes outlined in this chapter include communications, risks, stakeholder engagement, and the overall work.

4. Because culture is a resource that needs to be monitored just like any other resource, you believe the following areas or factors of the CMM Component Project deserve more attention and monitoring:

- Monitor how well the CMM team is drawing on or leveraging its current culture.

- Monitor how the team is shaping or changing its culture.

- Monitor to what extent differences are intentionally leveraged for good or take a back seat to achieving the CMM Project's goals and objectives.

- Confirm that the practice of assigning a person to a particular assignment has nothing to do with differences but rather with capabilities, maturity, and attitude.

- Confirm in cases where someone has infringed upon another's rights or created a less than safe work environment that our CMM PMO took swift steps to address the problem and set a positive example.

Chapter 12 Answers. Confirming Value, Closing, and Next Steps

1. The CMM Component Project team could prove useful being re-purposed to deliver the new 4th Component Project. In this way, the team should be able to more quickly deliver value than a newly assembled team could deliver.

2. The current S4V Component Project team could provide value by iterating on or improving the capabilities of the current solution for its existing user community, by adding capabilities or addressing Inclusive Design (usability gaps) of the current solution for a new user community, and by delivering on the expanded Charter to pursue Adjacent Spaces or Co-Innovation opportunities, address Minimalism goals, or seek out new value

by Mutating on More than One Gene or Regenerating through Combining.

3. With regard to archiving the CMM Component Project's knowledge, we first need to capture final Lessons Learned, and then we need to ensure all of the Project's learnings and knowledge maintained in the Knowledge Management system are archived for future reference and for use by others.

4. The PMO and relevant Stakeholders need to confirm that the Benefits Management Plan includes a Benefits Maximization plan (to ensure that the solution's benefits are expanded, extended, or otherwise maximized over time) and a Benefits Sustainment plan (to ensure that the solution's benefits do not disappear in the wake of Program/Project closure).

5. The six activities that need to be occur before staff can be released include capturing final lessons learned, archiving the Program's or Project's knowledge, completing and confirming completion of all planned work, performing remaining administrative tasks, obtaining formal signoff, and closing out any remaining contracts.

Appendix B

Design Thinking Techniques

There are literally hundreds of Design Thinking techniques. The ones outlined here have been shown to be useful for transformational Program and Project Management and have been applied in the book. We were tempted to organize these techniques around the steps or components of our *Design Thinking Model for Program and Project Management*, but in the end agreed that such an approach might actually be limiting. Instead each technique is arranged alphabetically. As you review this material, consider how each technique may be used *throughout* the Design Thinking process (*Understand-to-Deploy*) as well as *across* the Program and Project Management lifecycle (*Initiate-to-Close*) illustrated below.

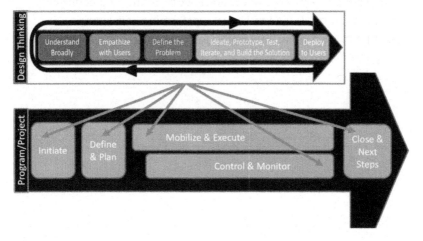

Adjacent Spaces. As we change anything in our Program or Project, consider how we can incrementally ease into the "white space" or conceptual adjacent space surrounding our current processes, methods, tools, and so on, with the idea that such change is more easily adopted or consumed because it is similar to what is currently in place. Said another way, use current strengths and capabilities to move into (or learn, or adopt) adjacent spaces. Such spaces could be technology-related, or reflect new business or application features, or represent new markets or processes, etc.

Aligning Strategy to Time Horizons. We need to think about today, the short-term, the mid-term, and the long-term, recognizing that our long-term vision must be prioritized to be realized (which in turn means that our short-term vision needs to blend the new with the current). Popular research suggests that the *mid-term* Time Horizon can be the most important, as it is often overlooked yet integral to achieving the long-term.

Artifact Chart. Details an artifact's or deliverable's primary and secondary audiences, goals, expected outcomes, and type of artifact (controlled, point-in-time, enduring, or living).

Backport into the Past. Consider how current innovations can be "backported" into current processes or businesses or organizations to give them new life. Get to the future faster by building upon what has already been built, in a way that affords greater time-to value at less cost and risk.

Backward Invention. Stripping out features to simplify a design or prototype (or that users do not want or find irritating).

Balance the Accidental with the Essential. With regard to complexity of an idea, design, interface, or deliverable, it is important to understand the complexity that can be removed vs the complexity that is necessary lest the idea, design, interface, or deliverable lose its value.

Brainstorming. A key ideation technique. To brainstorm effectively, consider the advice of the IDEO team below, simplified for our purposes here (https://www.ideou.com/pages/brainstorming):

> 1. Set the stage; frame the question to be stormed, share with the team what the research or experience tells us, and prepare the team to "embrace a mindset of curiosity."
>
> 2. Facilitate the brainstorming process; consider starting with a creative warm-up, then move into individual brainstorming, and then up-level the individual work to groups sharing their ideas and building on one another.
>
> 3. Follow-up; gather feedback and continue to incorporate new ideas through v-teams and communities.

Brainstorming in Reverse. Instead of trying to answer a question or think about a problem head-on, reverse the question or problem and have the team consider what would make things *worse*. Afterwards, "flip" the team's answers to think through answering the original question/problem (similar to the **Speedboat and Anchors** exercise where users assign problems or "anchors" to a situation or "speedboat").

Buddy System. The practice of pairing a new team member with a veteran team member for a period of time (such as the first month the new team member is on the Program or Project) to help answer onboarding questions, provide background data, and allow the new team member the chance to ease into their new role, the team's Work Climate, and an organization's overall culture. Though team-internal, the Buddy System shares some similarities with user Shadowing.

Build to Think. The notion that we may do our best ideation and thinking, and therefore arrive at solutions with improved time-to-value, when we simply jump in and start building or otherwise "doing." In contrast, for complex endeavors "planning to think" takes more time and will push many of our learnings late into the solutioning or testing process (where changes are expensive and ill-conceived designs head back to the drawing board).

CARMA Analysis. Use a cost and risk-modeled analysis to risk-weight, visualize, and assess architecture, staffing, development, testing, or other options to quantify an option's relative viability against other options; CARMA incorporates risk factors into traditional costing, using risk filters (option attributes) that increase or decrease option costs.

Cobb's Paradox and Matrix. Use Cobb's Paradox (which says "We know why projects fail; we know how to prevent their failure—so why do they still fail?") and Cobb's matrix/survey tool to think through and evaluate 10 specifically weighted user-centric, project management-centric, and other relevant factors or areas.

Co-Innovation. Develop solutions and deliverables together with users, partners, team members, or others in real-time side-by-side, rather than going back and forth between iterative defining, ideating, prototyping, demonstrating and testing, ideating again, eventually building the solution or deliverable, and so on.

Collaboration. Working with others to arrive at outcomes or execute in ways that would be difficult or impossible alone, with the understanding that no one does their best work, nor can difficult problems be solved, solo.

Crowd Sourcing. Gathering gratis thoughts, inputs, ideas, or potential solutions from a large group; a method for scaling collaboration beyond a small group, capitalizing on the thinking and capabilities of the *many*.

Culture Assessment. A tool or approach for assessing organizational or team culture across multiple values or dimensions (i.e. the Culture Cube) or layers (i.e. the Culture Onion).

Customer Journey Map. An illustration of the various touchpoints from beginning to end that together describe how a customer "flows" through their interaction with a product or service (Kelley & Kelley, 2013). Each touchpoint represents an opportunity to satisfy or disappoint a customer.

Day in the Life Analysis. Observing or recording the activities of a single (presumably) representative user to understand the nature of their work. The more repetitive the work, the more immediately useful this analysis; non-repetitive edge cases typically represent 10-20%.

Decision Authority Map. Visual mapping of Sponsors, stakeholders, leaders, subject matter experts, and other Program and Project team members who have been granted the *authority* to make decisions.

Defining the Problem. A key step in Design Thinking; research, ask probing questions, and employ the Five Why's. Draw on verbatims, stories, and other user feedback reflecting their challenges and pain points, and then frame the problem in the context of a specific Persona and Customer Journey Map. Employ deep and potentially divergent thinking techniques to arrive at the core problem (or first of the core problems). If we spend too little time understanding and defining the problem, we can easily find ourselves solving the wrong problem.

Demonstrations. Show mock-ups, prototypes, and other "demos" or ideas to others (team members and especially users) for the purpose of learning and course correcting and iterating.

Design Mindset. Centers around how something works; solution-focused rather than problem-focused. A design mindset requires a balance of cognitive analysis and imagination.

Design Thinking. A "human-centered approach to innovation that draws from the designer's toolkit to integrate the needs of people, the possibilities of technology, and the requirements for business success" (Brown, n.d.).

Divergent Thinking. Rather than trying to find the "right" answer to a problem, challenge current thinking (or ideas or designs) as a way to explore the surrounding situation; this is an effective way to gain broader understanding, define problems, promote empathy, and think through risks.

Diverse by Design. Build teams from the ground up with diversity in mind; consider how the availability and location of skills and capabilities, geographic and time zone implications, communications norms and minimum capabilities, and a myriad of cultural factors can aid or hinder creating balanced and diverse teams.

Edge Case Thinking. While edge cases are by definition rare in that they occur at extremes or boundaries, thinking through inevitable edge cases early helps provides insights into users who think, do, and consume systems and solutions differently than the majority. Such insights help us create smarter designs and solutions in the long run.

Empathizing. A key early step in Design Thinking; involves taking the steps necessary to more deeply understand another user, other person, or team. Synonymous with "walking in another's shoes" or "wearing another's hat."

Empathy Mapping. A process for learning about a specific Persona (a community or group of people who perform similar activities) by documenting how a user thinks and feels, what a user sees and hears or says and does, their biggest pain point, and their top one or two goals.

Empathy through Realized Changes. In Design Thinking, teams usually spend their time empathizing with users. In this case, however, we see users empathizing with the team seeking to help the users; the empathy comes as a result of realized changes and seeing real progress (no matter how small that progress might be). Thus, *empathy through realized changes* flips the user/team source/target relationship and flow of empathy.

Feedback Loop. One of the fundamentals of Design Thinking, create and employ feedback loops to apply learnings back into the initial problem, an idea, a design, a prototype, a test, and more.

Five Why's. An important method (and a staple of research) used for discovering the root cause or reasons behind a particular situation, line of thinking, decision, and other matters. This technique helps us understand user motivations, values, and biases as well. Ask "why" again and again to go beyond the obvious and explore the hidden.

Gamification. Build game design techniques into a prototype, pilot, or solution to drive engagement, incentivize new behaviors, and ultimately collect (more or richer) feedback.

Guiding Principles. Establish a lightweight set of foundational beliefs, rules, or behaviors that describe and explain "how" an organization or team should operate.

Good Enough. The notion that going beyond a design's, deliverable's, or solution's requirements is not only unnecessary but incredibly expensive from a diminishing returns perspective; increasing a deliverable's quality from 95% to 96% might double its cost or time-to-value, for example. Common practices (rather than best practices) are often executed to deliver "good enough" outcomes or other results.

Growth Mindset. Operating and thinking in a way that acknowledges learning requires trying and doing and also failing, and that failing is an important step on the journey to achievement. A growth mindset is incomplete without the ability to extend grace to others who are also learning and occasionally failing on their own knowledge journeys.

Hackathon. A scheduled sprint-like collaboration event used for brainstorming or more often for actually designing and building; may involve solution experts, business and technology professionals, project managers, interface subject matter experts, and other specialists.

Heatmap. A visualization of data or concepts comprising a complex landscape made simpler through the use of color (or sometimes other identifying marks, particularly in the context of inclusive design). The variety and gradation of color or other markings helps illustrate status or changes, and therefore helps draw attention to those changes. The chapter-specific content Figures found at the start of Chapters four through 12 are examples of simple heatmaps.

Ideate. The general process or mindset for thinking, imagining, learning, and ultimately identifying potential answers to questions. Ideation can be performed singularly or as part of a broader collaboration. Common ideation techniques include Brainstorming, Reverse Brainstorming, and Mind Mapping.

Inclusive (or Sensitive) Design. Consider user community abilities, challenges, culture, values, lifestyle, and preferences; allow this knowledge to influence with whom we empathize and how and what we design and deliver.

Increase Shared Identity. The process of finding or creating common threads or themes between people and teams; increasing Shared Identity is useful for creating and sustaining shared visions, driving stronger collaboration, and intentional culture shaping.

Innovate. The process of identifying and capitalizing on (doing!) ideas that live at the intersection of business viability, human desirability and usability, and technical feasibility (http://thestrategyguysite.com).

Inverse Power Law. The idea of introducing a high number of little changes, a fewer number of medium changes, and only a very few number of major changes (just as we observe in biology and nature, i.e. earthquake frequencies or changes in an ecosystem). If the frequency of our changes fails to map well to this Law, it is likely we are taking on too much change at once (which might be fine but could warrant how we plan, think, prepare, execute, or otherwise operate).

Iterate and **Iterations.** Perhaps the greatest value found in Design Thinking is to build upon, refine, or otherwise iterate on something already built, akin to standing on the Shoulders of Giants to reach another level of capability or usability.

Lessons Learned. A core Design Thinking method for incorporating learnings and feedback into future work. To be of use, learnings and knowledge must be captured regularly in a Lessons Learned Register throughout (rather than exclusively at the end of) Programs/Projects.

Mind Map. A visual method of exploring and broadly understanding a central idea by linking a second tier of other ideas or attributes or dependencies to it, followed by linking additional ideas to the second tier, and so on. As we branch out from the central idea, the mind map reveals a hierarchy or set of dependencies and other considerations illuminating that central idea. Mind maps are useful to better understand ideas, concepts, problems, prototype features, potential solution challenges, stakeholder relationships, deliverables structure, and required content.

Minimalism. The notion that the bare essentials are adequate. Minimalism is often seen as a goal for a *subset* of a user community that does not need all the bells and whistles of a complex user interface (or document or Plan, etc) but rather only needs a button or two (or a briefing, or a simple *strawman,* etc) to do their work.

Minimize the Variables. Avoid the temptation to take on or change too many things at once; you need to be able to manage the "new" while you preserve the "core."

Minimum Viable Product (MVP). The minimum level of functionality or capability that delivers value to users, with the understanding that the MVP must continue evolving through additional iterations to become the full-fledged solution envisioned or required in the first place.

Mock-Up. A lightweight prototype of a conceptual solution or design created for experimentation and visualization purposes. Mock-ups are often simple drawings or arrangements of diagram and pictures, or a partial replica of a larger whole, created for our purposes here using commonly available tools such as Microsoft PowerPoint, Word, Excel, or a whiteboard.

Modular Thinking and Building. Whether a design, prototype, or organizational structure, the idea is to build and think in modules that can later be recombined to create new capabilities, artifacts, or value.

Mutate on More than One Gene. With regard to introducing change to a product, service, solution, or prototype, avoid the tendency to focus on changing a single dimension or *mutating a single gene* over and over. Instead, mix things up and introduce change (one at a time) that involves mutating other genes.

Next Step Thinking. Prior to Program or Project closing, consider how to use the assembled team, their solution and processes, and their efficacy track record to deliver additional or new value beyond what has already been delivered (or on the path to be delivered).

Pattern. A high-level blueprint or design useful as a guide for future work; the conceptual version of a (standardized or other) template.

Persona Analysis. Create fictional characters (such as "finance user," "sales user," PMO users, specific document or artifact users, and other such amalgamations) to represent types or subsets of a user community who share common needs and will use specific artifacts or features of a solution or deliverable in similar ways.

Piloting. The idea of putting forth an early version of a solution for (typically) a subset of users to utilize for feedback purposes as well as productive use; pilots are more functionally complete than prototypes.

Postmortem. The practice of looking back in time to examine and dissect how a situation or problem arose, progressed, and concluded; also called a backbrief, and synonymous with lessons learned though the postmortem connotation typically implies a one-time examination at the end of a Program or Project.

Premortems. The "pre" version of a postmortem or backbrief, a premortem is performed to purposely think ahead about what might fail or occur, and why, *before such failures occur.* Premortems include building in mitigations or additional user involvement to avoid these failure scenarios. Premortems can help us identify and subsequently avoid the kind of fantastic failures that otherwise surprise and shut down Programs and Projects while also helping us see biases at work (i.e. confirmation bias or group think).

Principle of "No Surprises." When it comes to user interfaces, artifacts, standard documents, status reports, and other outcomes, users should not have to struggle with *how* to use, read, or otherwise consume them. Design should delight, be intuitive, and make matters clear rather than surprise or confuse. Apply this technique to communications, too, including escalating issues and potential risks early to stakeholders.

Probing for Understanding. Investigating and asking questions of users and others that cannot be answered without some thought. The goal of Probing is to bring clarity to a situation (whether current or potential) to avoid mistakes that have been made before and to find a way through the ambiguity ahead of us. Probing questions must also go beyond those questions that only clarify, though, and seek to understand the *edges* through open-ended "Why...?" and similar lines of questioning.

Proof of Concept. A limited prototype or exercise used to demonstrate that a particular capability or feature set is directionally aligned with user needs. A Proof of Concept exercise demonstrates feasibility.

Prototyping. The process of "building to think" by creating a solution (or partial solution) to a problem which may then be shared with users, tested, and iteratively refined (or tossed out); the idea is to learn fast, fail fast, iterate, and therefore make meaningful progress while learning and failing cheaply.

Rapid Prototyping. The process of quickly putting together a visualization of a potential solution to determine if the prototype is directionally accurate. Examples could be as simple as a whiteboard diagram, animated PowerPoint, or software-based wire-frame.

Regenerating through Combining. Consider how we can combine the old with the new in a modular way, the outcome of which is naturally "less new" and therefore more consumable.

Retrospective. Another form of lessons learned or learning from the past as past events and situations are observed in hindsight.

Scaling for Effectiveness. Consider the best way to scale the work or effort in front of you, using either a highly repeatable replication or *franchise* approach or an intentionally varied or *boutique* approach.

Silent Design. Learn and gather feedback by observing the changes that users (not designers!) make to a situation or solution to increase its effectiveness or usability after it has been deployed.

Simple Rules. A set of six or fewer Rules that describe who and what you are as a team or organization; may include what you do and don't do, outputs, priorities, boundaries; stop and start parameters, and more.

Shadowing. The process of following or working side-by-side with a user to understand their work first-hand. Shadowing can be extended (and made much more repeatable) by recording standard processes or step-by-step instructions.

Speedboat and Anchors Exercise. A method of Reverse Brainstorming where the brainstorming participants assign problems or *anchors* to a situation or *speedboat* with the intention of identifying what will slow down the speedboat. After the initial exercise, "flip" the logic to consider how to remove the anchors or transform them into speed enablers.

Stakeholder Map (and Register). The map is a visual or graphic representation of the register, including specific people, roles, and groups that have a stake or interest in Program/Project outcomes. The map and/or register are organized around users, Sponsors, leaders, partners, and the various teams required to design, develop, test, deploy, and operate a solution or product, and they include contact information, engagement dates, assessments of power and influence, and classifications and interests of each stakeholder. Maps and registers are not precisely interchangeable, but they both reflect similar data.

Standardized Template. A document organized in an empathy-aligned and structured way for a set of well-understood users. Standardized templates are intended for repeatable purposes; use a Standardized Template to build artifacts with consistency and to help ensure nothing content-wise is missed.

Storyboarding. A step-wise set of rough figures or drawings used to illustrate a sequence or set of steps in a process. Each figure is a step.

Story Telling. A communications and change management method that yields emotionally sticky and memorable outcomes by uniting the right (creative) side of the brain with the left (logic) side. Stories help messages resonate in ways that other communications mediums cannot. Good stories educate and change people and their attitudes, biases, and thinking, ultimately influencing work climate and culture.

Structured Text. Using words rather than pictures; considers how formatting, physical placement, margins and other whitespace, and text highlighting and color are used to drive consumability and elicit meaning.

The Rule of Threes. A prototype, new design, solution, deliverable, or other work product is rarely successful out of the gate; set expectations that it often takes three iterations to meet minimum requirements.

Time Pacing. Solutions exhibit rhythms in use. Understanding the peaks and valleys of a solution's utilization helps you thoughtfully structure staffing and deployment changes and create the most effective/least impactful rollout strategies.

Tossing out Traditional Strategies. Introduce Design Thinking when we identify untenable or dead-end traditional strategies such as *defending our position* when that position drives little value, or investing in *protecting a sacred cow* when it is time to let the market drive those economics, or *leveraging our core competencies* when those competencies have become less relevant.

Understand Broadly. A key first step in the *Design Thinking process for Program and Project Management*, understanding broadly involves assessing and learning the broader macro-environment within which a user or community operates.

User-Centric (or User-Centered or Human-Centered) Thinking. A general term synonymous with Design Thinking, where understanding the needs of a user or user community in the context of a specific environment drives empathy and ultimately better problem definition and solutioning.

User Engagement Metrics. As we work through empathizing and testing (and later, as we deploy and operationalize), we need to track how well our users believe we are engaging them and ask them what we need to do differently to be more user-centric.

References

Aaslaid, K. (2018). *50 Examples of Corporations That Failed to Innovate*. Retrieved from https://valuer.ai/blog/50-examples-of-corporations-that-failed-to-innovate-and-missed-their-chance/.

Alie, S. S. (2015). *Project governance: #1 critical success factor.* Paper presented at PMI® Global Congress 2015—Orlando, FL. Newtown Square, PA: Project Management Institute.

Anderson, G., Nilson, C., et al. (2009). *SAP Implementation Unleashed: A Business and Technical Roadmap to Deploying SAP*. Indianapolis: SAMS Publishing.

Anderson, G. (2010). Using CARMA to communicate the value of EA designs, *IASA Perspectives* (Fall 2010).

Anitha, J., & Begum, F. (2016). Role of organizational culture and employee commitment in employee retention. *ASBM Journal of Management,* 9(1), 17-28. Retrieved June 27, 2019, from https://www.questia.com/ library/journal/1P3-3964279081/role-of-organisational-culture-and-employee-commitment.

Ben Mahmoud-Jouini, S., Midler, C., & Silberzahn, P. (2016). Contributions of design thinking to project management in an innovation context. *Project Management Journal*, 47(2),144-156.

Berman, E. M. (2006). *Performance and productivity in public and nonprofit organizations (2nd ed.)*. NY, NY: Routledge.

Brown, T. (n.d.). *Why Design Thinking*. Retrieved May 6, 2019, from https://www.ideou.com/pages/design-thinking.

Brown, T. (2019). *Change by Design: How Design Thinking Transforms Organizations and Inspires Innovation*. NY, NY: HarperBusiness.

Cobb, M. (1995). *Unfinished Voyages*. Presentation at The CHAOS University, sponsored by The Standish Group, Nov 6-9, 1995. Chatham, MA.

Flemming, L. (2007). Breakthroughs and the "Long Tail" of Innovation. *Sloan Management Review*. 49(1), 69-74 + 93.

Elmansy, R. (2017). *Ideation in Design Thinking: Tools and Methods*. Retrieved June 8, 2019, from https://www.designorate.com/ideation-design-thinking-tools/.

Elmansy, R. (2018). *Why Design Thinking Doesn't Work*. Retrieved June 1, 2019, from https://www.designorate.com/why-design-thinking-doesnt-work/.

Forbes. (2011, July). Global Diversity and Inclusion: Fostering Innovation Through a Diverse Workforce. *Forbes Insight Report*. Retrieved April 19, 2019, from https://i.forbesimg.com/forbesinsights/StudyPDFs /Innovation_Through_Diversity.pdf.

Furino, R. (2016). *Getting your Project Team ready to be ready*. Retrieved April 30, 2019, from https://www.linkedin.com/pulse/getting-your-project-team-ready-richard-furino/.

Furino, R. (2016). *Stakeholder Engagement: A very human endeavor*. Paper presented at PMI® North America Congress—San Diego, CA: Project Management Institute (September 25-28).

Gay, B. (2019). *Adoption of Design Thinking*. Retrieved July 5, 2019, from https://brucegay.com/2019/04/27/adoption-of-design-thinking/.

Gibbings, M. (2018). Are you outsourcing your change leadership? *Governance Directions*,70(8), 506-510.

Goleman, D. (2017). *What Makes a Leader?* Harvard Business Review Classics. Boston, MA: HBR Press.

Graziano, M. (2019). 5 Double-edged sword Philosophies that lead to Destructive Company Culture: Understanding the Barriers to High Performance. *Leadership Excellence*, 36(5), 33-35. Retrieved July 21, 2019, from https://hr.com/.

Greer, L. L., de Jong, B. A., Schouten, M. E. & Dannals, J. E. (2018). Why and When Hierarchy Impacts Team Effectiveness: A Meta-Analytic Integration, *Journal of Applied Psychology*, 103, 591-613.

Heathfield, S. (2012). *How to Change Your Culture: Organizational Culture Change.* Retrieved August 23, 2019, from http://www.execterim.com/pdf/Organizationalculturechange.pdf.

Herold, M., Kearl S., Aksut, A., & Vupasi, M. T. (2019). *Building a Recurring Revenue Management Solution in Dynamics 365: A Design Thinking Approach*. Paper presented at Winter Ready, Feb 11-15, Seattle, WA.

Kahneman, D. (2011). *Thinking, Fast and Slow.* NY, NY: Farrar, Straus and Giroux.

Kaushik, S. (2015). *Project Management using Design Thinking*. Retrieved June 22, 2019, from https://www.slideshare.net/ saurabhkaushikin/design-thinking-introduction-47596844.

Kelley, D., & Kelley, T. (2013). *Creative Confidence: Unleashing the Creative Potential within us All.* NY, NY: Crown Business.

Nadella, S. (2017). *Hit Refresh: The Quest to Rediscover Microsoft's Soul and Imagine a Better Future for Everyone*. NY, NY: HarperCollins.

Patnaik, D. (2012). *Innovation Starts with Empathy.* Retrieved May 20, 2018, from http://www.jumpassociates.com/learning-posts/innovation-starts-with-empathy/.

Petrone, P. (2017). *The Most Common Mistakes Leaders Make When Communicating Change*. Retrieved April 21, 2019, from https://learning.linkedin.com/blog/ learning-tips/the-most-common-mistakes-leaders-make-handling-change.

Pink, D. H. (2009). *Drive: The Surprising Truth About What Motivates Us*. NY, NY: Riverhead Hardcover.

Project Management Institute. (2017). *A Guide to the Project Management Body of Knowledge (PMBOK® Guide)—Sixth Edition*. Newtown Square, PA: Author.

Project Management Institute. (2019). *Program Management Professional (PgMP) Handbook*. Newtown Square, PA: Author.

Rittel, Horst W. J.; Webber, Melvin M. (1973). Dilemmas in a General Theory of Planning. *Policy Sciences*. 4 (2): 155–169.

Schein, E. H. (2010). *Organizational Culture and Leadership*. NY, NY: Jossey-Bass.

Tyler, C. F. (2019). The Rise Of Empathetic Leadership. *Leadership Excellence, 36*(5), 8-9.

FEEDBACK TO THE AUTHOR

Consistent with Design Thinking, the author invites you to please send your feedback to him at George.Anderson@Microsoft.com. The goal is to iterate on and refine this material; remember the **Rule of Threes**!

Feedback is only limited by your imagination. Please highlight gaps in the material including additional **Design Thinking** techniques you have found useful on large-scale complex or unique Programs and Projects. Call out your criticisms, note any sentence and grammar issues however small, and share your thoughts for updated figures, new figures, and other diagrams.

Also, please highlight any redundancies and inconsistencies. More importantly, highlight opportunities to go deeper or to explore additional Program and Project Management **Adjacent Spaces** and other areas. Share what you like as well, including how you have used the material here as-is *and* how you have applied or intend to apply **Silent Design** to improve the material's usefulness. In doing all of this, know that your **Co-Innovation** time and feedback are vastly appreciated.

Made in the USA
Las Vegas, NV
15 December 2021

38008329R00116